AF251693

SS REGALIA

SS REGALIA

Jack Pia

ISBN 0-345-29449-1

Manufactured in the United States of America

First Edition: June 1974

9 8 7 6 5 4 3 2

Contents

Introduction

It has come to seem characteristic of the most powerful and pervasive organisations of the twentieth century that they chose to cloak their identity in the anonymity of abbreviations and acronyms — Cheka, Ogpu, NKVD, KGB, Gestapo. Of these shorthand symbols, none is better known, or more redolent of menace, than the two letters SS. They stand at once for naked power and for secret violence, for the shouts of propaganda and the whispers of intrigue, for the drumbeats of Nuremberg and the knock on the door in the night-time, for defeat or victory on world battlefields and for squalid alleyway scuffles, for the burial mounds of Nordic heroes and for the mass graves of six million innocent victims. That the image of the SS is so multiform, that it chose to become both a public and an invisible power in Nazi Germany makes it quite different from most of those other organs of espionage and repression under which the peoples of Europe have suffered in the last fifty years. To understand the nature and role of any and all of them requires the most delicate and perceptive enquiry into the power structure of a totalitarian state; but to understand the SS requires as well an insight into the popular mind of Nazi Germany, into the function which myth and legend, folklore and folk history had in its working, into the influence which symbol and imagery exerted on its philosophy and outlook.

But though the SS became many things, the first important fact to establish about it is that it began as a small and very simple organisation: as a personal bodyguard to Hitler, the leader of the infant Nazi party, in the early days of the *Kampfzeit* — the struggle for power. It was with him during the Munich putsch in November 1923, when it was known as the *Stosstrupp Adolf Hitler*, and five of its very small number were killed at his side on the Odeonsplatz. He reformed it when he re-emerged from prison in 1925, when it took the title *Schutzstaffel* (Defence Squad) under which it would later become notorious. And it shortly afterwards began to recruit members outside the immediate vicinity of the Führer's head-quarters. The idea which lay behind this, however, was only an extension of the bodyguard principle. It was to provide in each German city a small group of Nazis of proved toughness who would act in all circumstances out of total loyalty to the Führer, to protect if not his person then his interests within the party.

By 1930 it numbered still under three hundred. But in that year it was given a new leader who began at once to transform its structure and size, with an eye to making it the organ of ultimate power (subject only to Hitler's will) within the Nazi movement. The man was Heinrich Himmler, a young middle-class Bavarian, mild in appearance and modest in habits, whose weak chin and pince-nez were an unlikely facade for one of the most tubulent imaginations which the nineteenth or twentieth centuries has produced. For Himmler did not merely believe, he believed fervently and obsessively, in the whole stewpot of ideological, racial, nationalist, and patriotic notions from which Hitler ladled out his message to the German people. Racial superiority, eastward expansion, supermanhood, back-to-the-landism, rune reading, the cult of the open air, health faddery — Himmler was not merely to preach all these as fundamental truths of thought or action; where appropriate, he practised them himself. To one, however, he held more strongly than to any and, in the SS, he was to find certainly the ideal, perhaps the only, setting in which he might put it into practice. The 'truth' was that of racial superiority, the superiority of the 'pure Aryan' over other peoples, and of the German Aryan above all. The SS had always been choosy about its membership, but its criteria of selection had been hitherto essentially practical : was the candidate amenable to discipline, fit, tough, sober, trust-worthy? To these criteria Himmler now added another : could he show untainted (ie non-Jewish, non-Slav) descent for three generations? (Later the period of qualification was to be progressively pushed back into the eighteenth, and then into the seventeenth century.) If not, he could not join. And indeed Himmler was eventually to expel from the SS, established members whose genealogy was found not to meet the standards he had laid down for new members.

But the racial purification process was, initially at least, to be gradual. The first three years of Himmler's command were given over to a struggle for survival against, and then for mastery over, the other para-military organisation within the Nazi movement, the Sturmabteilungen (SA). The SS had long been counted a component of the SA, though Himmler was able to minimize its subordinate status, but the guiding principle of the two bodies had always diverged. The SA wanted mass membership, since Röhm, its leader, foresaw it as the People's Army which would replace the *Reichswehr* after the battle for power had been won (and which might strike to win that battle by violence in the streets if Hitler's 'constitutional' approach looked in danger of foundering). Hitler was desperately anxious, throughout the years 1930–33, that its power be kept in check, since open acts of armed defiance against the Weimar republic would provide the government with exactly the sort of pretext on which it might move to suppress his party, and count on the army to obey its orders. His dilemma was, therefore, that he needed the demonstration of mob support which the SA lent his party but he also needed it to be law-abiding. The agent which could assure this difficult balance of forces was to be the SS, which under Himmler's leadership turned into a sort of party police force, and one with several important successes to its record.

Confronted by an unruly mass movement, Himmler naturally postponed the imposition of his selection standards in favour of attracting numbers. And during the few months on each side of the Seizure of Power in January 1933, new members flowed to him in quantity; they, the 'March Violets', had sensed that it was Himmler, not Röhm, who was driving the bandwaggon. After Himmler's bloody triumph over Röhm, in the purge of 30th June 1934, he was however to institute a major weeding-out of 'unworthy' members, which fell particularly heavily on the old ex-Free Corps men who had lent it muscle in the difficult days.

Himmler could afford these expulsions because, after 1934, he began to add enormously to the range of functions which the SS performed and to the responsibilities it carried. In that year the SS established two of its most important branches: the military SS and the concentration camp guards. The first, to become known in 1940 as the Waffen SS, appeared in the form of a personal guard regiment for the Führer, the *Leibstandarte Adolf Hitler*. Commanded by one of his old *barbouzes*, Sepp Dietrich, it had begun as a headquarter guard in Munich but was to grow henceforth into the élite of one of the most ruthless and dedicated military organisations ever known. The second, the *Totenkopfverbände*, had its origin in SS detachments assigned to run the quite illegal *ad hoc* prisons set up by the regime in 1933 to house its political opponents. In 1936, Himmler achieved what was to be perhaps the most significant of all his accretions of power, nomination as Chief of German Police. Through possession of that office he combined under his control the SS's own Security Service (Sicherheitsdienst – SD), the Prussian Secret

State Police, the Gestapo, which he had taken over three years earlier, the Criminal Police, and the ordinary uniformed police forces of the town and countryside. Only with the creation of the extermination units — *Einsatzgruppen* — in 1942 and the capture in 1944 of the Wehrmacht's counter-espionage service, the *Abwehr*, would he add sensibly to his apparatus of repression and terror.

The increasingly institutional and full-time character of the SS did not mean however that membership was no longer open after 1933 to the ordinary party member. Provided he was judged suitable — or useful — the SS welcomed his candidature as before. But the part-time membership was hived off after the Seizure of Power into what became known as the *Allgemeine* (General) SS, a body without functions — except those of providing money and recruits to the active branches.

Whether full- or part-time, however, all wore the same uniform, accoutrements and badges. The basic colour, of course, was black, which had featured in the rig-out of the original *Stosstrupp* and had been formally adopted in 1930. The choice was not arbitrary, for the colour had important overtones in Germany. Many of the *Freischutzen* who had led the resistance to Napoleon in the War of Liberation of 1813–15 had worn it, and it was the predominant colour of the uniforms of some of the most distinguished cavalry regiments of the Kaiser's army, notably the 1st and 2nd *Leib-Husaren* (the 'Death's Head Hussars', of which more later). It is too obvious to note that Mussolini had already made it the Fascist colour; but, as Andrew Mollo points out in 'Military Fashion,' he may have done so for a now forgotten reason: the adoption of black by a number of all-officer units of the anti-Red armies in the Russian civil war. It was this, he suggests, which initially imbued the colour with a political meaning. However, it is realistic to recognise that the deliberate choice of colour for some symbolic purpose is always heavily influenced by un-conscious factors, both by those which the chooser wishes to play upon the minds of others, and those at work in his own. The SS leadership may very well therefore have calculated that black is popularly associated with mystery and danger, with winter and midnight; did they also call to mind that it is the colour of the sorcerer's cloak, of the witch's hat, of the vest-ments of those who worship the devil himself in the ceremony of the black mass? One supposes not; but it is by no means unconvincing to suggest that these magical and demonic echoes played their part in the process which clothed the SS in their sinister and distinctive hue.

The range of symbols used to decorate and distinguish rank and categories on the SS uniform seems to have been arrived at by the same interplay of conscious and unconscious choice. The SS collar runes, commonly described as the 'double lightning flash', harked back, in a half-educated way, to the Nordic past in which Himmler believed he would have felt so much at home. The oakleaf and the acorn were emblematic of the First German Empire, whose shadowy and questionable glories Himmler wished the SS to re-create. The Death's Head, besides its graveyard menace, was the famous badge of four vanished regiments of the Kaiser's army (the 92nd Brunswick Infantry and the 17th as well as the 1st and 2nd Hussars), while the wearing of a title on a cuff-ribbon, adopted during the First World War by the Richthofen and other fighter squadrons, had originated in the Xth (Hannover) Army Corps as a means of displaying the battle honours which the King's German Legion had won in the Napoleonic wars. The Xth Corps' right to do so was dubious, for it could show no descent from that distinguished army-in-exile which had served the English King George III as its own Elector of Hanover. But it pleased Kaiser Wilhelm's anglophilia to pretend otherwise, in the same way as it subsequently pleased the SS to mimic the appearance of his aerial aces. Mimicry of things English, it is possible to argue, may also have been a direct influence upon the cut and style of the SS uniform, for the collar and tie, Sam Browne belt, boots and breeches, the general silhouhette of the ensemble are highly reminiscent of the service dress of the British officer of the First World War; and it is now widely recognised that the fashion of victor-nations is one of the most powerful influences on changes in military costume, in the same way, by analogy, that hunting tribesmen adopt as apparel the skins of the animals most difficult and dangerous to kill.

But there was much that was deliberately and distinctively German in the SS style, particularly in the wearing of the forester's dagger which Himmler granted to the most favoured members of the order, of the sword designed to the traditional pattern of the *Reichswehr*, and in the eventual adoption of field-grey for the *Waffen* SS. It was perhaps in his schemes for the organisation of the *Waffen* SS that Himmler most success-fully made use of popular German historical memories, for the titles of its divisions are in almost every case a reminder of some important episode or hero of Germany's past: *Hohenstauffen, Frundsberg, Gotz von Berlechingen, Prinz Eugen, Reich, Leibstandarte* – all are words of power and influence. Beyond that, however, it is now possible to suggest that Himmler's resort to the use of individual titles and to the emphasis on unit identities was, in the national context, an extremely clever psychological stroke by a man striving to build up a large military force solely through the medium of voluntary enlistment. For the old Kaiser's army had been built on the principle of strong unit identity and on a hierarchy of regiments, with the Guards at the top. Hitler had deliberately reconstructed the *Wehrmacht* on a pattern which owed nothing to the past and made no differentiation between one unit and another, since he wanted the new army to be wholly and entirely his own. In fulfilling that wish, however, he undoubtedly frustrated a strongly-established element in the German attitude to military service. Himmler, by recognising the German soldier's inclination to belong to an identifiable and élite formation, certainly attracted many who would not otherwise have been drawn to so politically tainted an organisation.

But that assumption raises again the whole question of the role which the outward appearance of the SS played in furthering its status and influence within the Third Reich. Whatever the hidden or historical origins of the many elements which went to make up that appearance, the combined effect was both dramatic and menacing. To the initiate, the effect was heightened by the complicated system of badges of rank and distinction which each SS man wore in addition. It is one of the merits of this book that it both conveys the striking and particular quality of the SS uniform and catalogues in detail the minutiae of status-symbols, the award of which provided one of the mechanisms through which Himmler kept his strange and evil empire obedient to his will.

by John Keegan

Allgemeine ⚡⚡

Top left: Pair of collar patches of an SS Scharführer on the staff of the SS High Command, or the staff of an SS Oberabschnitt (Main District). *Top right:* Sleeve badge worn on the lower left sleeve above the cuffband by members of the Main Race and Settlement Department of the SS (Rasse and Siedlungs Hauptamt – RuS.Ha). This was one of the many departments that made up the Reichsfürung SS (RFSS – SS High Command). The badge was introduced on 6th October 1935. *Centre:* Cuffband worn on the lower left sleeve by non-commissioned members of the Main Race and Settlement Department of the SS. Introduced on 25th January 1935. *Bottom:* Cuffband worn by non-commissioned ranks on the staff of SS Oberabschnitt (Main District) Böhmen Mähren (Bohemia and Moravia—Czechoslovakia) formed during Spring/Summer 1944

Each SS Abschnitt had under its command two or more SS Standarten (Regiments). *Top:* Pair of collar patches of an SS Scharführer of SS Standarte (Regiment) No 10 (Neustadt, later Kaiserslautern). The collar patches have pre-October 1934 white twisted cord edging. *Centre:* Pair of collar patches of an SS Sturmmann of SS Standarte No 24 (Oldenburg). These have post-October 1934 black and silver twisted cord edging. *Bottom:* Pair of collar patches of an SS Unterscharführer of SS Standarte No 48 (Köln). Despite an order from Himmler stating that all non-commissioned ranks must wear collar patches embroidered in silver grey thread, and that only officers were permitted to wear aluminium embroidery, examples of collar patches in aluminium thread worn by non-commissioned ranks are by no means uncommon

SS Oberabschmitte (Main District) were each divided into two or more SS Abschnitte (Sub-Districts). Each Abschnitt had, in addition to a regular staff, an SS Sanitäts-Abteilung (Medical Detachment). *Top* Cuffband worn by officers on the staff of the medical detachment of SS Abschnitt XXXXIII. Medical cuffbands were introduced in 1935; until then members of medical units had worn the cuffband of the regular staff. However, this particular example dates from 1939 when SS Abschnitt XXXXIII was formed. *Bottom:* Cuffband worn by members of the staff of SS Abschnitt XXXXIII. This SS Abschnitt was a component unit of SS Oberabschnitt Warthe in Poland, and had its HQ in Litzmannstadt

Top: Collar patch of an SS Officer below the rank of SS Standartenführer (colonel) of SS Standarte No 112 (Litzmannstadt – Poland). *Bottom:* Pair of collar patches of an Ehrenführer (Honorary Officer) with the rank of colonel, attached to SS Standarte No 2 (Frankfurt/Main). Honorary officers in the SS were usually men of high position or wealth, whose influence could be useful to the SS. They had their own special rank insignia which was introduced in 1934 for a limited period and then abolished

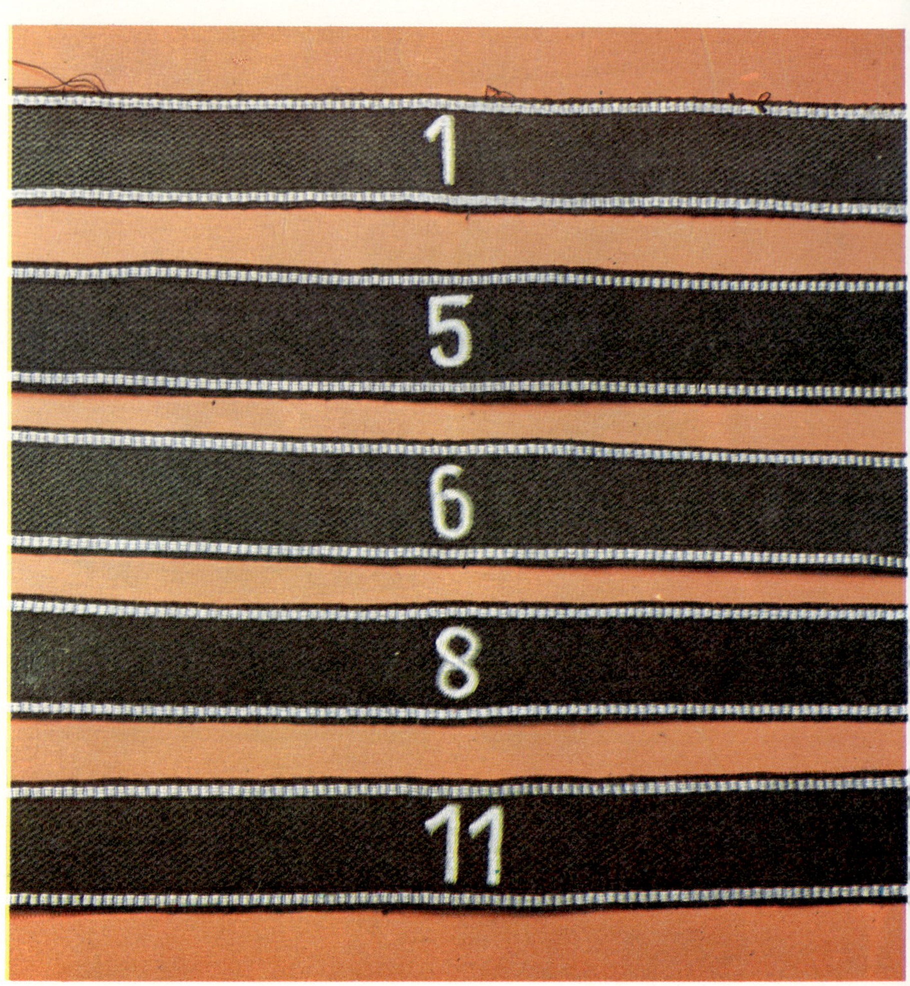

Cuffbands worn by officers on the staffs of SS Standarten (Regiments), the numeral on the cuffband denotes the numbers of the regiments as follows; *From top to bottom:* SS Standarte No 1 (Munich). This was worn until about 1935 when the regiment was named after Julius Schreck, one of the first SS men: SS Standarte No 5 (Koblenz, later Trier): SS Standarte No 6 (Berlin): SS Standarte No 8 (Liegnitz, Hirchberg later Tratenau): SS Standarte No 11 (Wien-Austria): Cuffbands of this pattern were also worn by the staff of SS motorized units in which case the numeral was also worn on the collar preceded by a large M

Each Allgemeine SS Regiment was divided into four regular, and one or more reserve battalions (Stürmbanne). Each Stürmbann was divided into four Stürme (Companies). On the cuffband the colour of the edges indicated the Stürmbann, and the numeral the Sturm. Until 1934, the colours were as follows:

Sturmbann I – green
Sturmbann II – dark blue
Sturmbann III – red
Sturmbann IV – light blue

The Sturme were numbered from No 1 in each Sturmbann, and these cuffbands could therefore be found with any numeral from one upwards according to the number of Sturme. After 1934 the system was changed as follows:

Sturmbann I – green edges   Sturme 1–4
Sturmbann II – dark blue   Sturme 5–7
Sturmbann III – red   Sturme 9–12
Sturmbann IV – dark red   Sturme 13–
Reserve Sturmbann light blue with Reserve and Sturm number

From top to bottom: Pre-1934 non-commissioned ranks cuffband, Sturmbann III, Sturm I: Pre-1934 officer's cuffband Sturmbann II Sturm 3 (This particular example originally had dark blue edges, which have faded owing to exposure to strong sunlight): Pre-1934 non-commissioned ranks cuffband, Sturmbann IV, Sturm 4: Pre-1934 cuffband for all ranks on the staff of Sturmbann·IV

Top: Pre-October 1934 collar patch, using hand-embroidered numerals and white twisted cord, worn by a non-commissioned member of SS Standarte No 28 (Hamburg). *Centre:* Pair of collar patches of an SS Unterscharführer of SS Standarte No 28 (Hamburg), produced with officer's quality embroidery. *Bottom:* Cuffband worn by officers on the staff of SS Standarte No 28 (Hamburg)

In addition to the units previously mentioned, the Allgemeine SS had specialist units at all levels.
Top: Pair of collar patches of an SS Oberscharführer in an SS engineer unit attached to the staff of an SS Oberabschnitt. *Centre:* Collar patches of a non-commissioned member of SS Signals Battalion No 6 (Hamburg), introduced 1st February 1934. *Bottom left:* Sleeve badge worn by officers of SS cavalry units, and cavalry schools. *Bottom centre:* Sleeve badge worn by SS signal officers. *Bottom right:* Sleeve badge worn by non-commissioned signallers

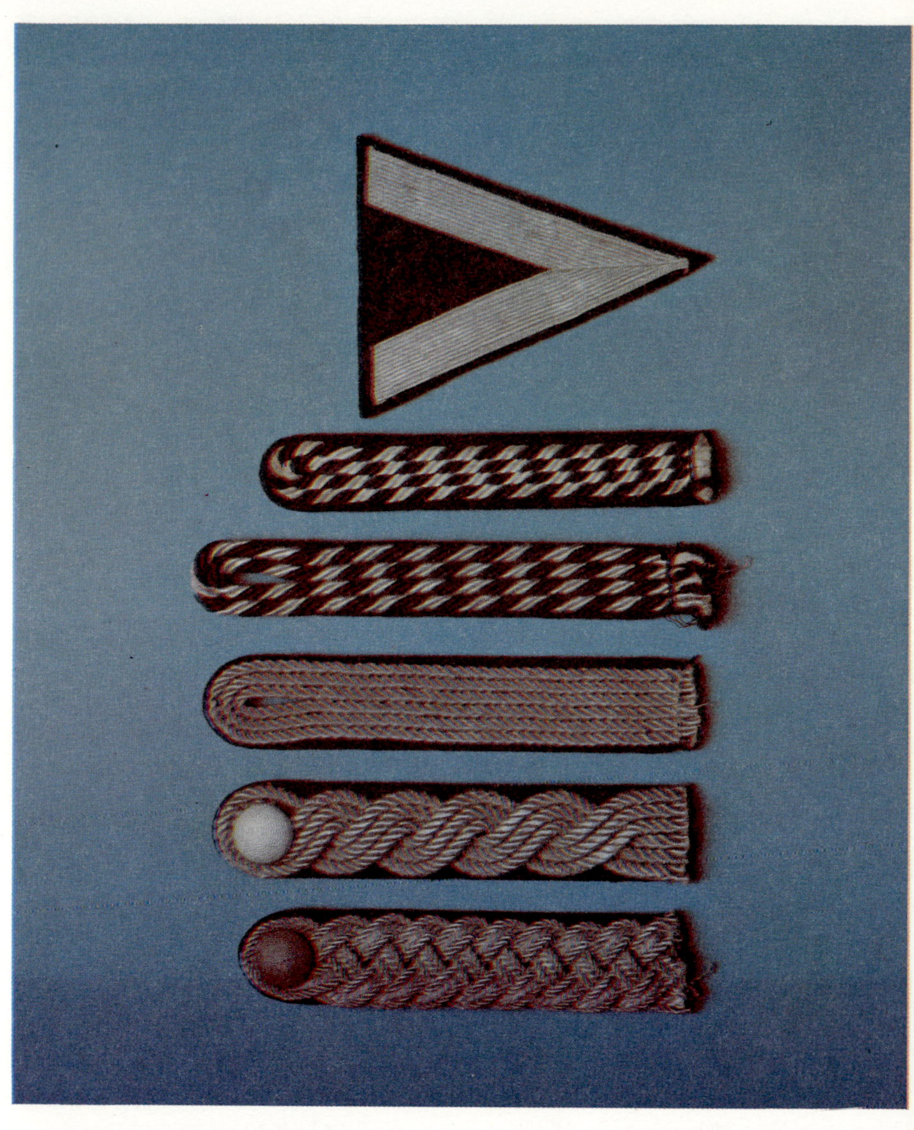

From top to bottom: Chevron worn on lower right sleeve by SS Stabsscharführer: Non-commissioned ranks shoulder strap worn from 15th May to October 1934: Non-commissioned ranks shoulder strap worn from 12th December 1934: Shoulder strap introduced 15th May 1934 for SS Untersturmführer up to and including SS Hauptsturmführer: Shoulder strap introduced 15th May 1934 for SS Sturmbannführer up to and including SS Standartenführer: Shoulder strap introduced 15th May 1934 for SS Oberführer up to and including SS Obergruppenführer. In 1942 a further rank, SS Oberstgruppenführer, was introduced, which also wore the above shoulder strap. (The shoulder strap worn by Heinrich Himmler as Reichsführer SS was identical to the above, but after August 1934 an oak leaf spray in white metal was worn in the centre.)

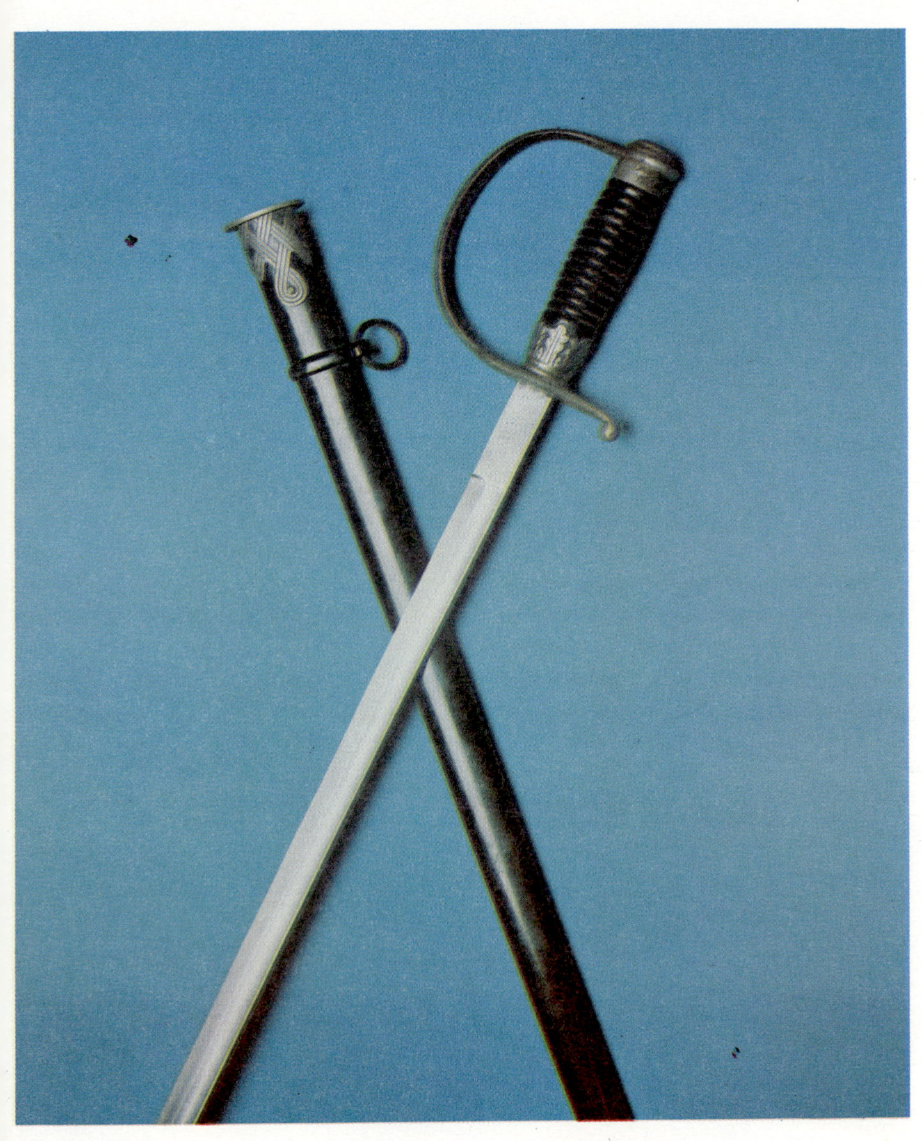

SS NCO's sword

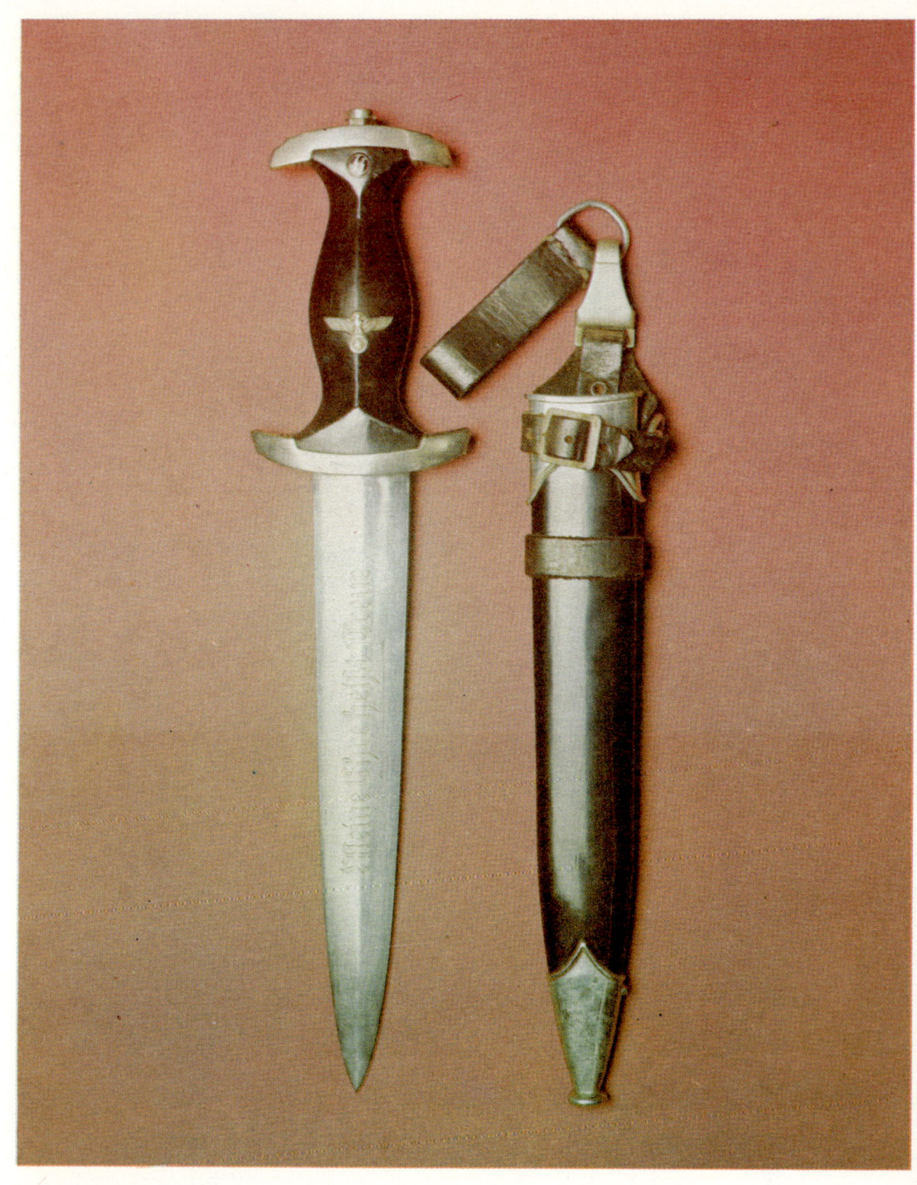

SS Service dagger, 1933 model, for all ranks in general SS after three years as an SS candidate and having been accepted in the SS

SS Service dagger, 1936 model, worn by commissioned and non-commissioned personnel. Sheath fitting and chain hanger differ from 1933 model

Top: Armband regulation other ranks pattern. Armband was worn on black and earth grey uniforms (black edges band) although not apparent from the armband, this was worn by a member of the 1st Company of the 6th Allgemeine Standarte (Spandau): *Bottom:* Armband non-regulation variation (without black edges). Although RZM regulations decreed that all armbands should have black edges, this example is in fact marked by the RZM and another example is known to exist in a private collection. RZM – Reichszeugmeisterei (Central Ordnance Office of Nazi Party), established in the early 1930s and responsible for uniformity and quality control of all Nazi regalia; the armed forces did not come under these regulations

Top: Armband worn on black and earth grey uniforms. This particular example bears the unit stamp of 28th SS Motorised Unit (Allgemeine SS). *Bottom:* Armband worn on greatcoat

Top left: SS Shooting Award 2nd Class. *Top right:* SS Shooting Award 1st Class. *Centre:* Badge worn by non-commissioned ranks on upper left sleeve of fencing jacket. *Bottom left:* Badge worn on lower left sleeve by non-commissioned ranks who were qualified veterinary surgeons. *Bottom right:* Officers in the legal service. These were usually attached to the SS Hauptamt which was a department of the SS High Command. Introduced 20th March 1938

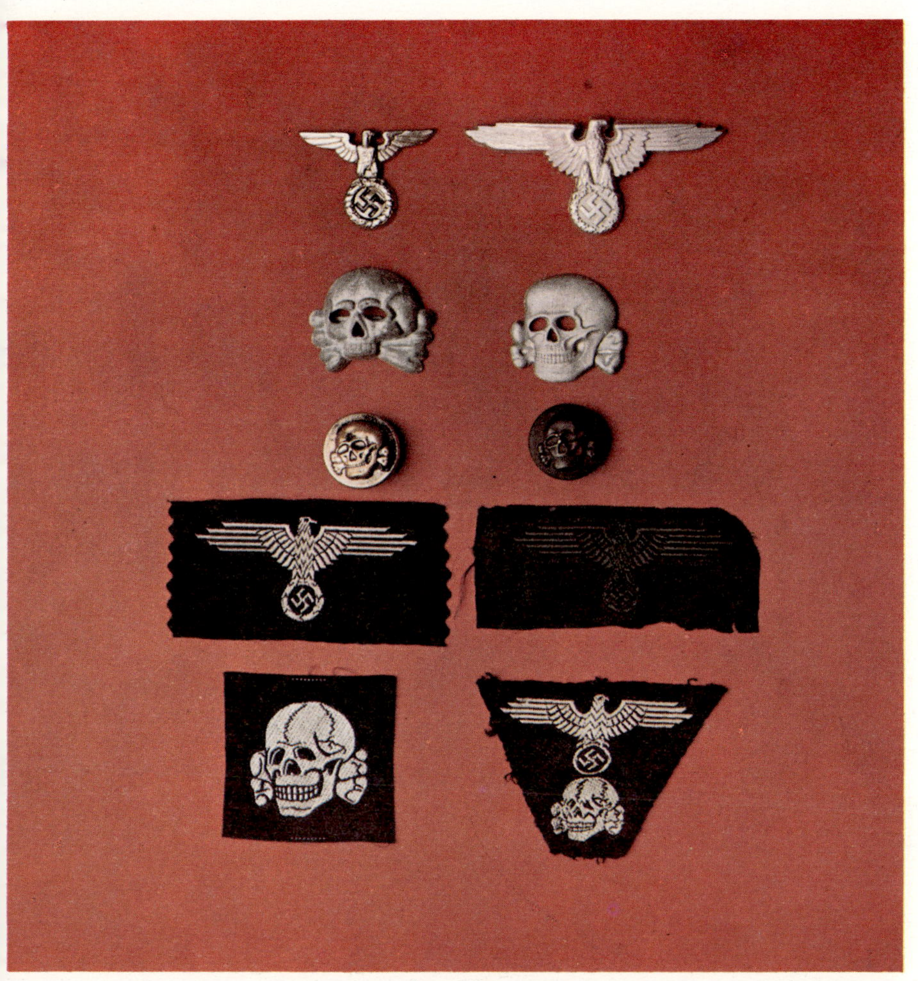

Top row left: First pattern SS cap eagle 1929–1936. *Top row right:* First pattern Death's Head 1923–1934. *Second row left:* Second pattern cap eagle 1936–1934. *Second row right:* Second pattern Death's Head 1934–1945. *Third row left:* Death's Head button in white metal for first pattern field cap 1932–1934. *Third row right:* Death's Head button for field grey field-cap 1935–1939. (Death's Head button was worn on front of cap and machine-embroidered eagle was worn on left side of the cap.) *Fourth row left:* Other ranks field-cap eagle 1939–1945. *Fourth row right:* Other ranks field-cap Death's Head 1939–1945. *Bottom row left:* Variation of No 7 worn on spring pattern camouflaged caps. *Bottom row right:* Insignia worn on 1943 pattern SS field-cap

SS   Kepi worn with traditional uniform in about 1934.

Lebensborn Society belt buckle. Thought to be unofficial, possibly worn by female staff at one of the Lebensborn homes

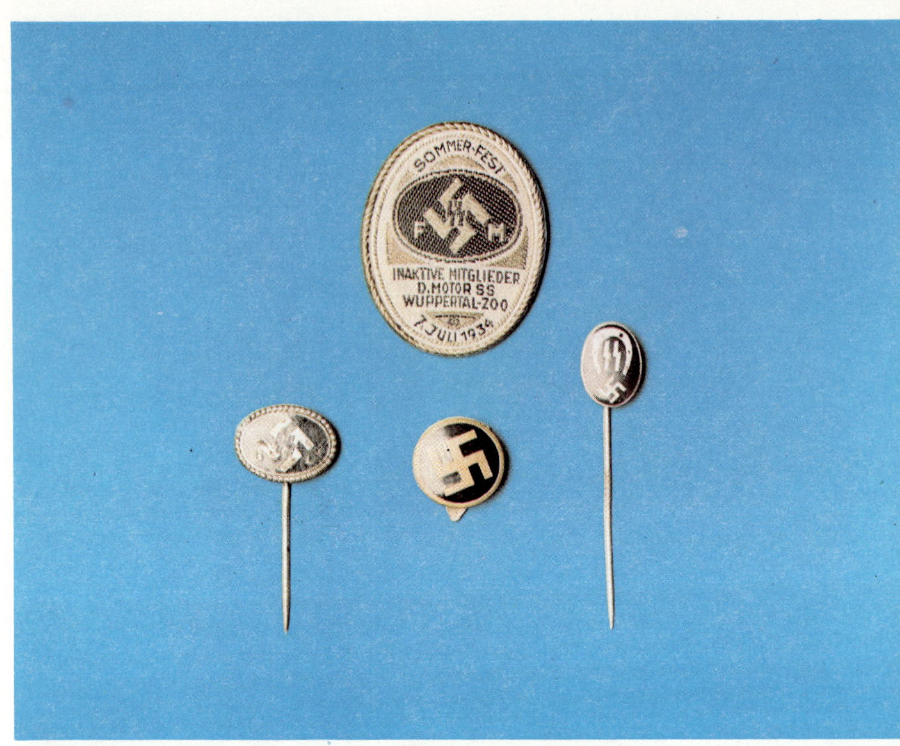

SS lapel badges

Top: Rally badge commemorating the summer festival of supporting members of the Motorised SS in Wuppertal-Zoo, 7th July 1934. *Below left:* Lapel badge worn by supporting members of the Dutch SS. *Below centre:* Lapel badge worn by members of the Flemish SS in civilian clothes. *Below right:* Lapel badge worn by members of SS cavalry units in civilian clothes (unofficial)

Left: SS supporting member's commemorative badge. *Centre:* SS supporting member's badge. *Right:* Badge to commemorate 5th anniversary of raising of the SS unit in the Chemnitz area

Das Schwarze Korps (the black corps), the official newspaper of the SS 1935–1945

Allgemeine SS Mann Regiment No 82 (Bielefeld), 8th Company 2nd Battalion — in black service dress, about May 1934. Black service dress was introduced in 1932 but was not formalised until late 1934. Compare this tunic with regulation tunic in preceding item — note detailed variation in shape of pocket flaps and in particular three buttons and absence of black stripes on swastika armband.

Traditional uniform: formalised by 1932 and last worn in summer of 1936. The uniform shown here is that of an SS Mann on the staff of a main department or district; about 1933–34.

Close-up of SS issue tie showing NSDAP party badge. Nazi Party membership badge when worn with a uniform was worn on the tie, and on the lapel with civilian clothes

Allgemeine SS Mann. SS Regiment No 4 (Hamburg), 5th Company 2nd Battalion, about 1936. In full black service dress with full marching equipment.

Back view showing fur-covered pack with rolled greatcoat, groundsheet and mess tin. The dagger is suspended from belt by vertical hanger; introduced in 1934. Also on belt is bread bag and water bottle. Black service dress is regulation pattern.

Earth grey drill service dress for NCOs; 1st Company 1st Battalion Allgemeine Regiment No 24 Sturmann. Introduced 25th May 1934.

Close-up showing dagger suspended from loop under pocket flap in undress uniform worn with long earth grey trousers on off-duty occasions.

Standard of the Hitler Bodyguard Regiment 'SS Adolf Hitler'

Standard of the SS Regiment 'Julius Schreck (Munich)'

Both sides of an SS trumpet banner

Evening dress for senior members of the SS

Waffen SS

Waffen SS collar patches

Top: Pair of collar patches of an SS Scharführer. Plain black unit patches were worn by many of the foreign volunteer units before they were given their own national emblems. *Bottom left:* Collar patch worn by other ranks in SS Regiment 1 'Deutschland' (although initially part of the SS Verfugungstruppe, the Deutschland regiment wore this insignia in the early war years when they were officially designed Waffen SS). *Bottom right:* Collar patch worn by members of 15th Waffen Grenadier Division der SS (Lettische No 1) (Latvian)

SS Officers' insignia

Top: Embroidered sleeve eagle worn by all officers on the left sleeve. This was largely replaced by a machine woven version in 1939. *Centre:* Pair of collar patches of an SS Gruppenführer, post-1942 pattern. Rank insignia was worn on both patches by SS Standartenführer (Colonel and above). *Bottom:* Pair of collar patches of an SS Sturmbannführer in the Waffen SS

From top to bottom: Waffen SS other ranks regulation pattern cuffband. 2nd SS Panzer Division Das Reich: Officer's band non-regulation pattern. 4th SS Polizei Panzer Grenadier Division pattern: Other ranks regulation cuffband. 9th Panzer Division 'Hohenstaufen': Other ranks regulation pattern cuffband 16th SS Panzer Division 'Frundsberg'

Top centre: Waffen SS officer's collar patch. Worn in all German units of the Waffen SS with the exception of police and Death's Head units. Two shoulder straps. *Top left:* Early pattern. *Top right:* Late pattern. Worn by all ranks up to Rottenführer (approximately corporal). 1st SS Panzer Division, Leibstandarte 'Adolf Hitler'. Colour of piping denotes armoured service (faded with age on this example): light blue—supply units, administrative and technical services. Golden yellow—cavalry and reconnaissance. *Bottom:* Officer's cuffband. 1st SS Panzer Division Leibstandarte 'Adolf Hitler' (regulation pattern)

Note: Cuffband worn on lower left sleeve. Collar patch worn up to rank of colonel. Unit is shown on left collar patch. Rank is shown on right collar patch

Top: SS Runic collar patch 'Bevo' pattern worn by German units of Waffen SS. *Centre:* Shoulder strap worn by SS-Unterführer-Anwärter (signed for 12 years' service) of the 1st SS Panzer Division, Leibstandarte 'Adolf Hitler'. *Bottom:* Non-regulation other ranks cuffband 1st SS Panzer Division, Leibstandarte 'Adolf Hitler'

Top left: Other ranks Runic collar patch worn by all German Waffen SS units except for Death's Head formations. *Top right:* Other ranks collar patch worn by Waffen SS formations. This is the early version of the Death's Head. *Centre and bottom:* Officer's cuffband SS VT Regiment 1 'Deutschland'; *centre* is gothic lettering, *bottom* is block lettering (later variety). This regiment later became part of the 2nd SS Panzer Division 'Das Reich'

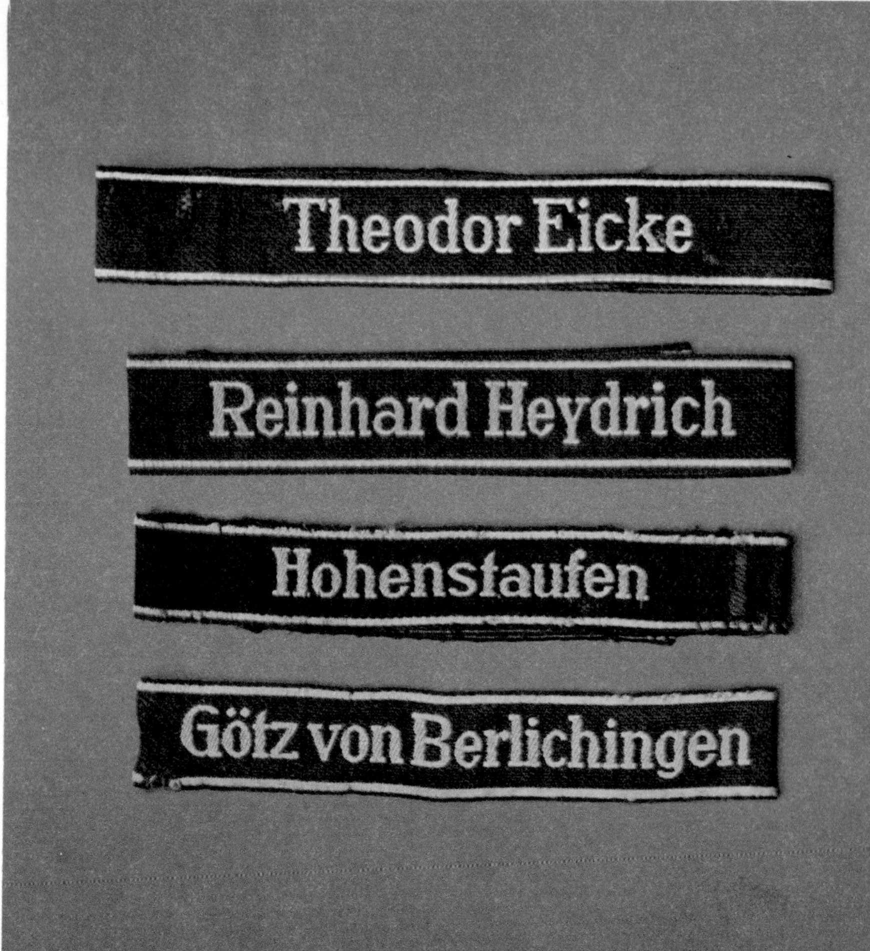

From top to bottom: Theodore Eicke 3rd SS Totenkopf Grenadier Standarte, later 6th SS Panzer Grenadier Regiment, of 3rd SS Panzer Division 'Totenkopf': With effect from 2nd March 1943, the 3rd SS Totenkopf-Grenadier Standarte received the honorary title 'Theodore Eicke', after the first commander of the 'Totenkopf' Division who was killed in action in Russia on 26th February 1943. 3rd SS Totenkopf Grenadier Standarte later became SS Panzer Grenadier Regiment No 6, 'Theodor Eicke': 'Reinhard Heydrich'. 11th SS Gebirgsjäger Regiment of 6 SS Gebirgs-Division 'Nord': Authorised on 4th June 1942, this cuffband bore the name of the former leader of the SS Security Service (Sicherheitsdienst-SD) who was assassinated in Czeckoslovakia in 1942: Divisional cuffband 9th SS Panzer Division 'Hohenstaufen': Divisional cuffband 17th SS Panzer Grenadier Division 'Götz von Berlichingen'.

Top left: Other ranks collar patch 14th Waffen Grenadier Division der SS Galizische No 1. *Top right:* Other ranks collar patch of 19th Waffen Grenadier Division der SS (Lettische No 2). *Centre:* Armshield worn by Lithuanian volunteers, army pattern. *Centre:* Other ranks cuffband 5th SS Panzer Division 'Wiking'. *Bottom:* Cuffband worn by other ranks SS-Freiwilligen-Grenadier-Division 'Langemarck'. This cuffband is a locally produced variation

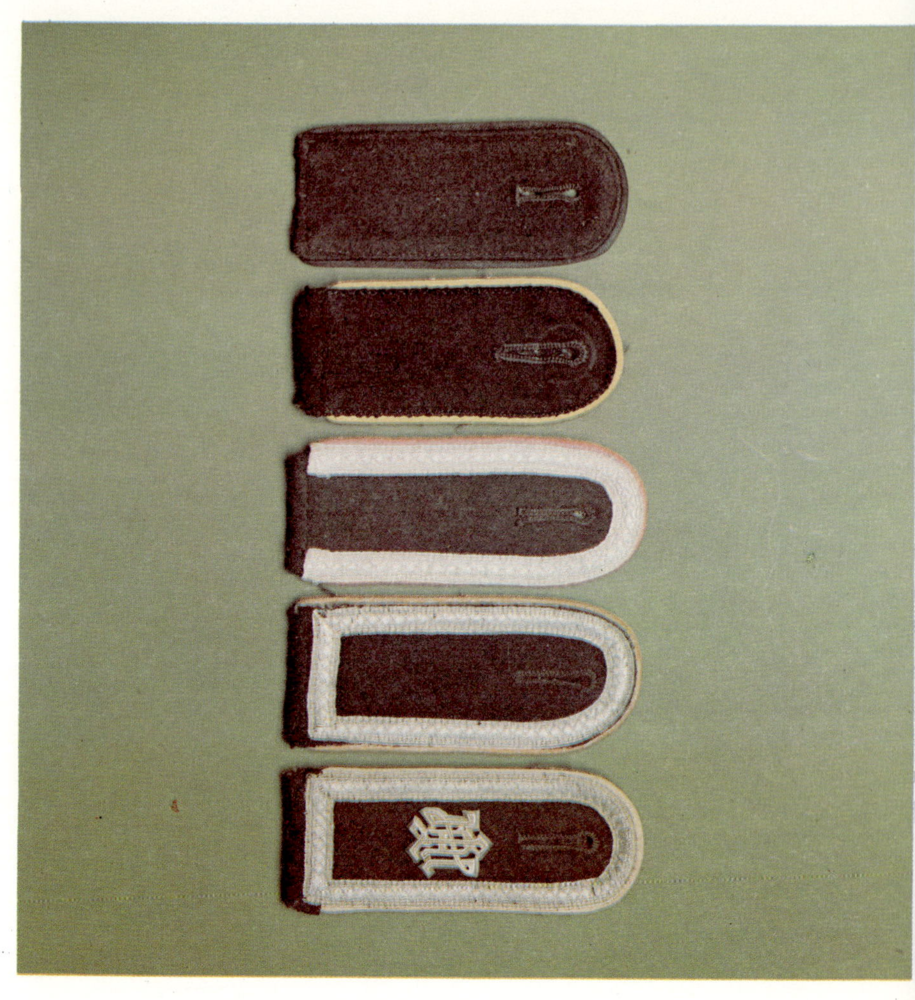

Waffen SS other ranks shoulder straps
SS Schutze (private)-Rottenführer (Engineers): SS Schutze (private) (Signals): SS Unterscharführer (Panzer):
SS Scharführer (Infantry with LAH monogram)

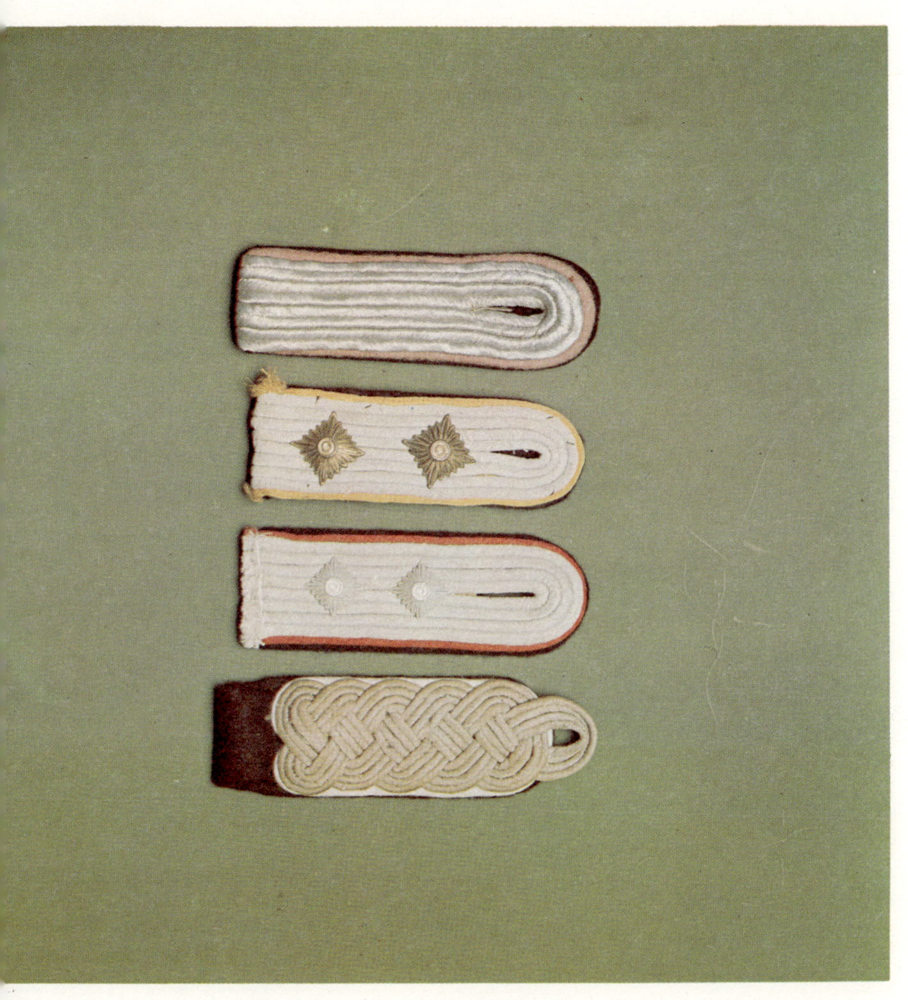

Waffen SS Officers' shoulder straps

SS Untersturmführer (Panzer): SS Hauptsturmführer (Cavalry, early pattern gilt pips): SS Hauptscharführer (Artillery):
SS Sturmbannführer (Infantry)

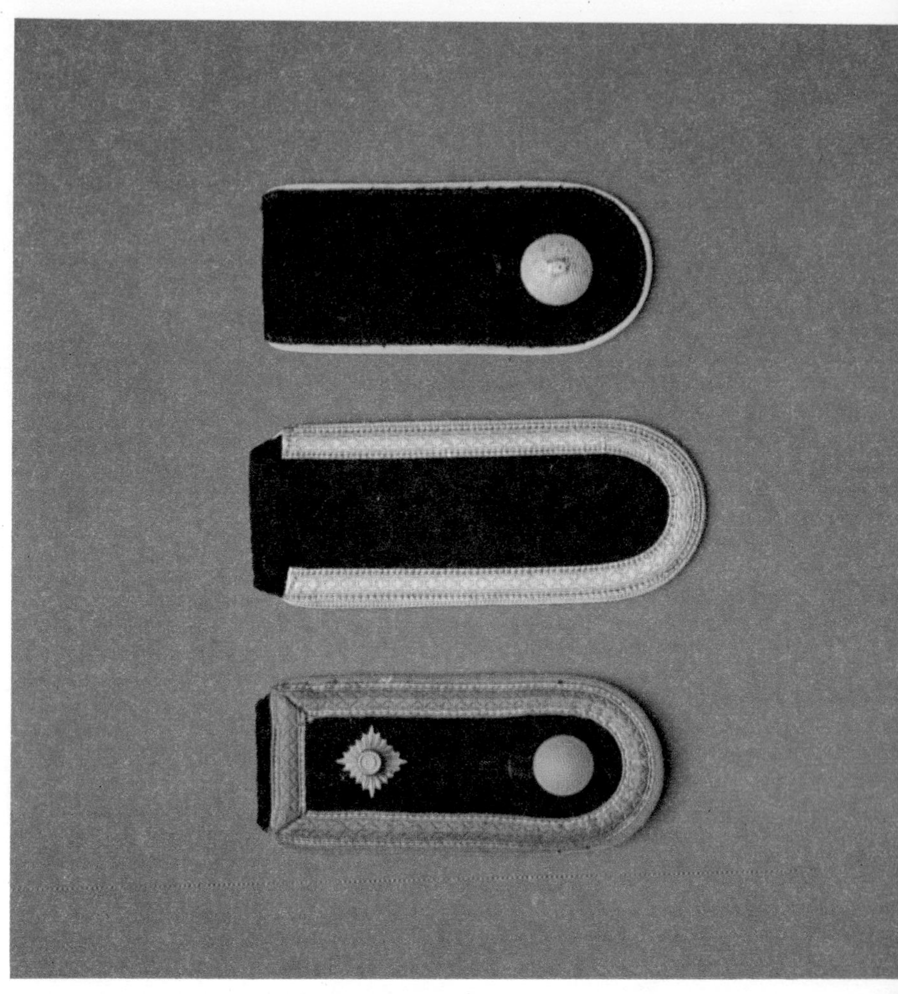

Other ranks and NCOs, Waffen SS
Top: SS Mann up to and including SS Rottenführer: white piping denotes infantry. *Middle:* SS Unterscharführer: white piping denotes infantry. *Bottom:* SS Oberscharführer: pink piping denotes SS Panzer

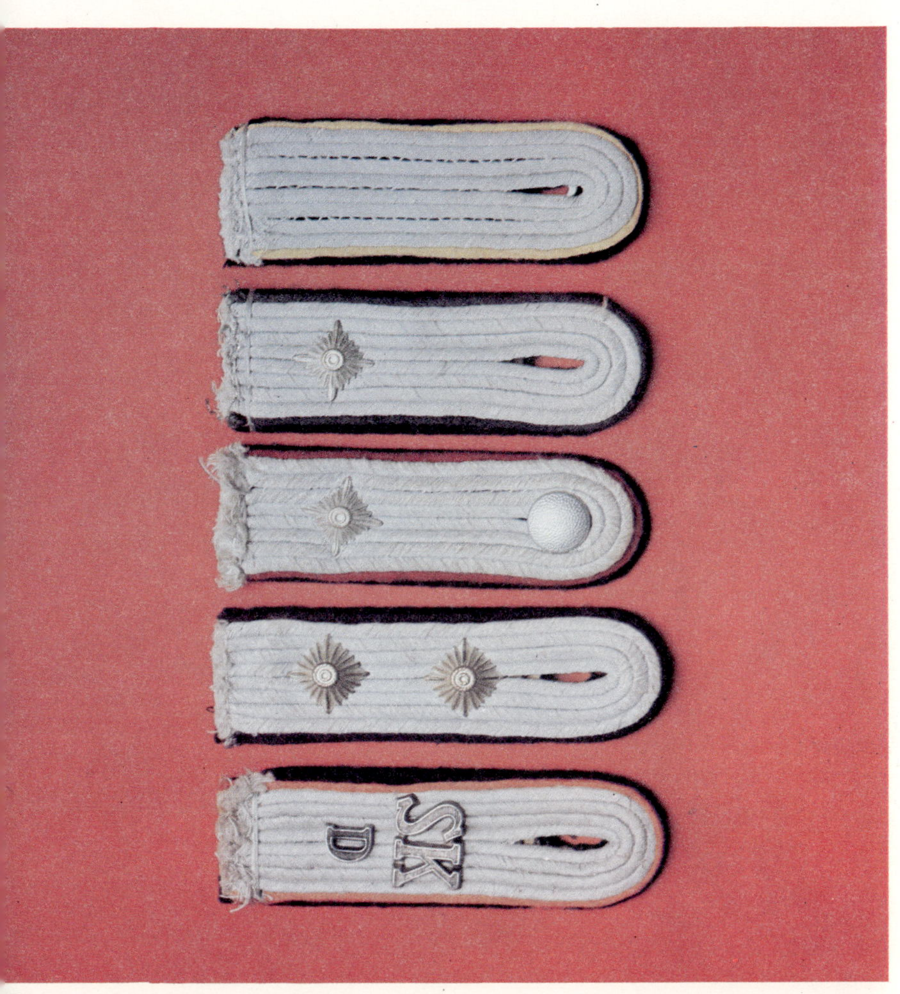

SS Officers' shoulder straps. *From top to bottom:*

SS Untersturmführer; pale yellow denotes signal troops and warcorrespondents in propaganda companies:

SS Obersturmführer reserve officers and officers for special employment. These are specialists within the Waffen SS given the status of an officer: SS Obersturmführer artillery and anti-aircraft artillery: Hauptsturmführer in the engineers: Untersturmführer Sonder-Kommando Dauchau-SS military police units in the Dauchau military complex

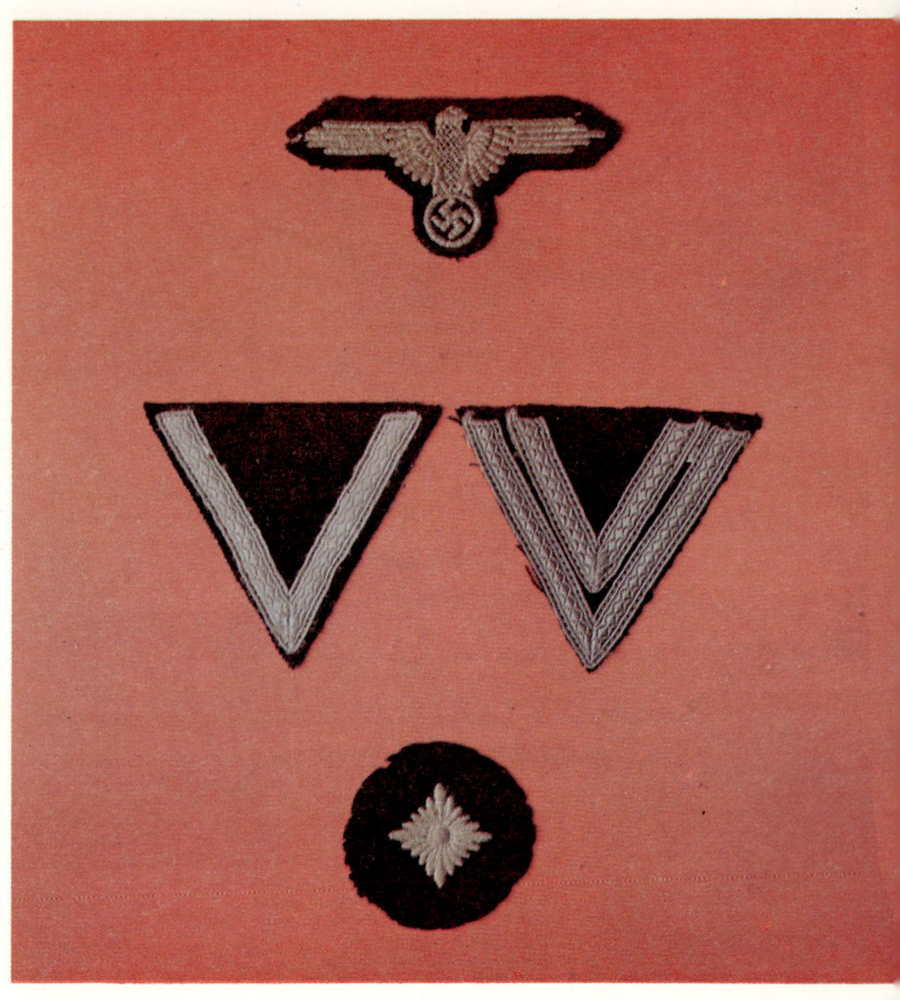

Top: Sleeve eagle worn by all other ranks in the Waffen SS on left sleeve. *Centre left:* Ranks chevron. SS Sturmmann. *Centre right:* SS Rottenführer. *Bottom:* SS Oberschütze. All three badges worn on left sleeve immediately below sleeve eagle.

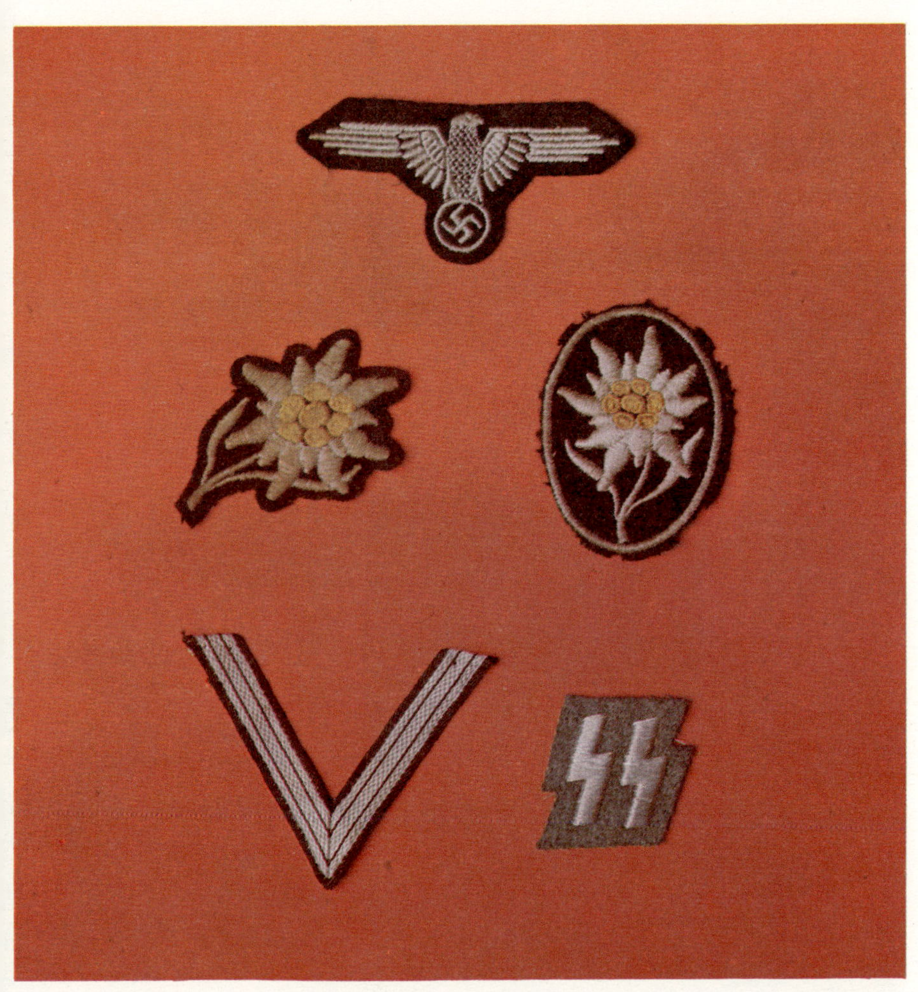

Top: Sleeve eagle worn by other ranks in the Waffen SS. *Centre left:* Edelweiss worn on left side of field cap by all ranks of mountain units of the Waffen SS. *Centre right:* Edelweiss worn on right sleeve by all ranks of mountain units of Waffen SS. *Bottom left:* 'Old Fighters' chevron worn on upper right sleeves by SS men who were members of the SS NSDAP or any other Nazi organisation before 30th January 1933. When worn in conjunction with sleeve edelweiss the base of Edelweiss badge came two centimetres below the level of the top of the 'V'. *Bottom right:* SS Runes worn immediately below left breast pocket on the police uniform by all members of the police who were also full members of the SS and on the Waffen SS uniform by all German-born members of the Waffen SS serving with foreign volunteer units which had their own distinctive collar patch

Top: Waffen SS other ranks late pattern collar patch, 3rd SS Panzer Division 'Totenkopf' and Death's Head units. Other ranks shoulder straps. Colour of piping denotes armoured service. *Bottom left:* White: Corps Divisional HQ staff. Also infantry and grenadiers Oberscharführer (approximately sergeant). *Bottom centre:* Red: Artillery including artillery schools and anti-aircraft artillery. All ranks up to SS Rottenführer. *Bottom right:* Pink: Tank and anti-tank units, rank as above. Probably a greatcoat shoulder strap because of its length

Foreign volunteer armshields worn by foreign personnel serving in armed forces. Although not strictly SS, all the foreign volunteers were drafted into the SS by 1943–44 and in many cases wore their original army insignia

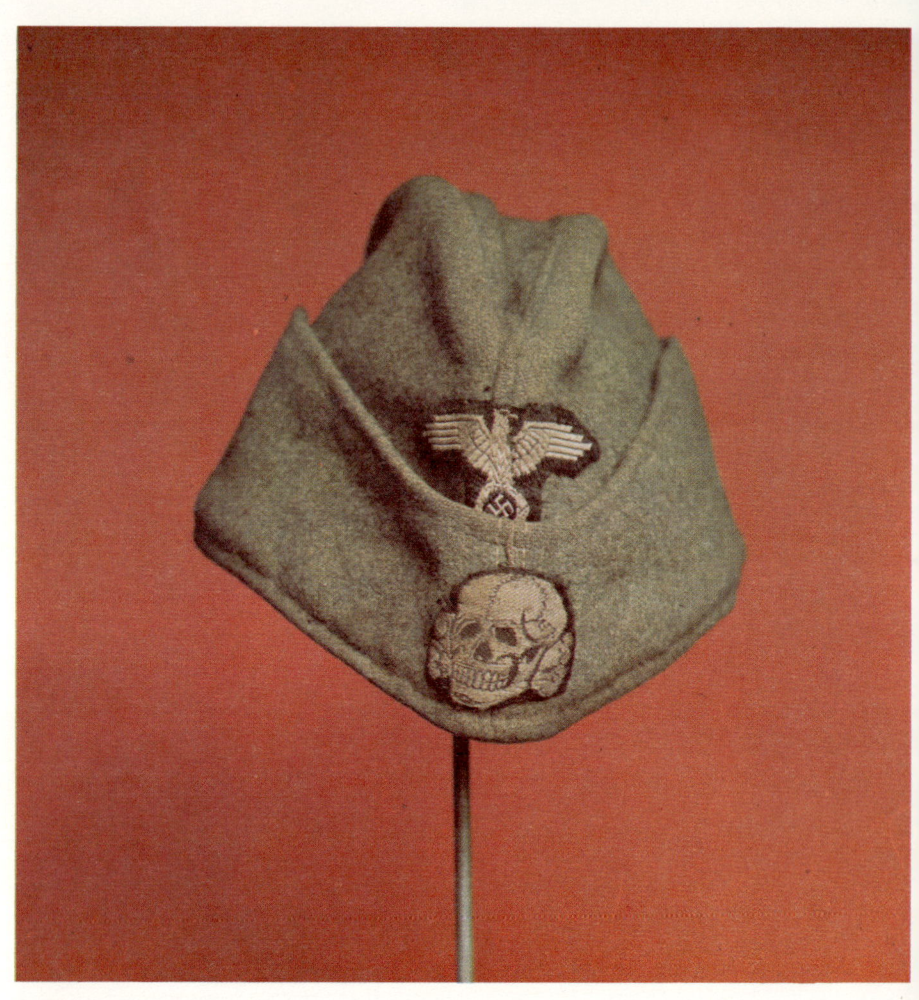

Waffen SS NCO's early pattern field cap. The white piping denotes infantry

Waffen SS other ranks' and NCO's field cap of about 1940

Waffen SS Rottenführer in full marching order. 2nd SS Panzer Division 'Das Reich,' about 1942. The red piping on shoulder strap indicates artillery. Note reversible camouflaged shelter quarter shown on pack showing spring camouflage

Reverse of opposite page

Waffen SS Rottenführer in spring camouflage smock with field equipment, about 1940. Note fighting knife often worn tucked in top of uniform, and stick grenade in belt

Reverse of opposite page: The Waffen SS was the first military unit to be issued with camouflaged clothing on an organisational basis

Waffen SS autumn-winter camouflage consisting of smock hood and gauntlets. The gauntlets make provision for trigger finger and thumb

SS triangular shelter quarter worn as a poncho showing autumn camouflage

Waffen SS Rottenführer in camouflage unit introduced in 1944

Special pattern Panzer jacket worn by an SS private. The yellow piping on the shoulder strap shows that the wearer was a member of a Panzer signal unit

Uniform of an SS Mann (private) in the 1st SS Panzer Division Leibstandarte SS 'Adolf Hitler'. Clearly visible are the 'slip on' LAH monograms on his shoulder straps. This is the 1943 pattern tunic

Wooden handled fighting knife. The scabbard is fitted with spring-loaded hook to fit on to any part of equipment

Left: SS officer's sword knot. *Right:* SS other ranks' sword knot

SS vehicle pennant with weatherproof cover

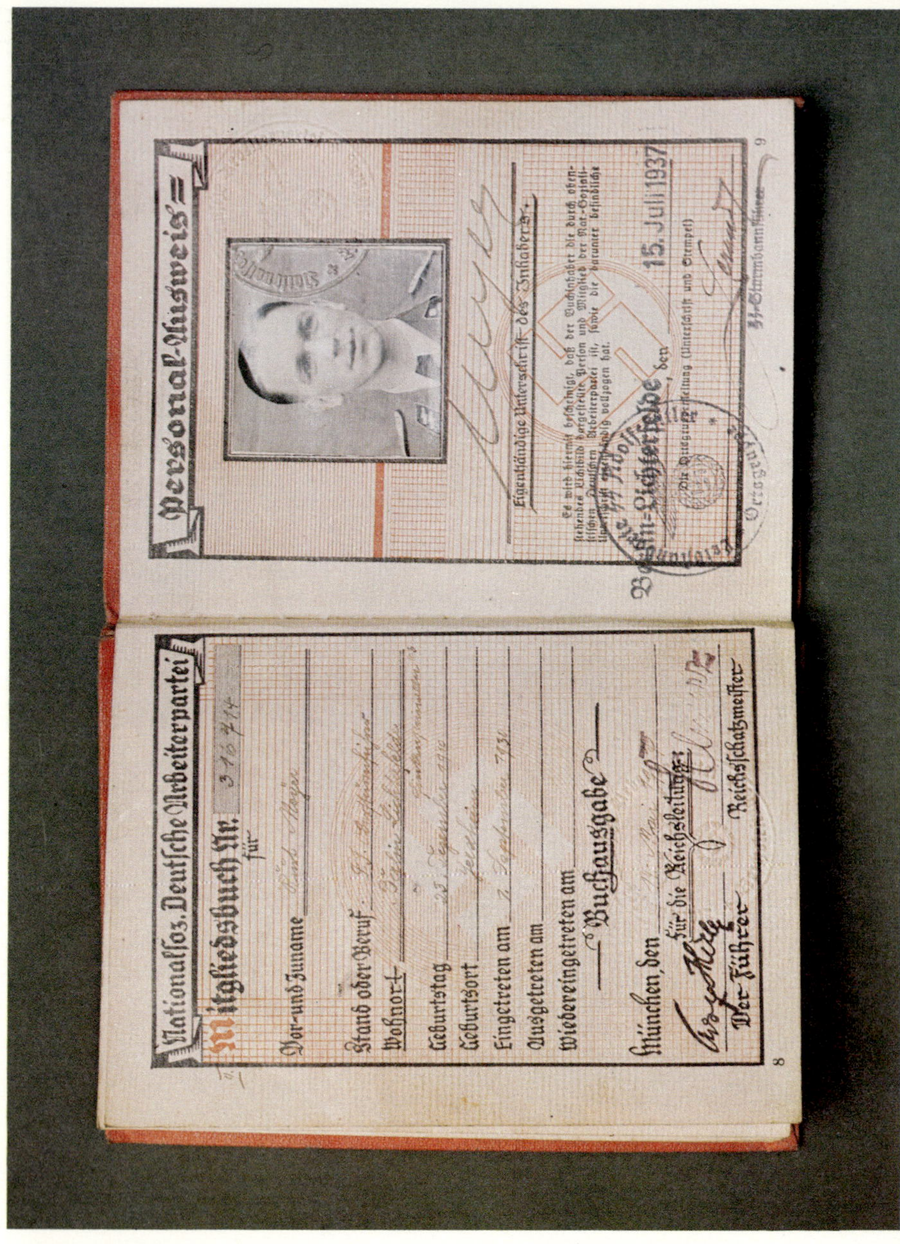

Party Membership book belonging to Kurt Meyer. At this time he was a member of the Leibstandarte SS 'Adolf Hitler.' He later became the commander of the 13th SS Panzer Division 'Hitler Jugend.' He was also the youngest general in the Waffen SS. He earned the nickname 'Panzer Meyer' for outstanding achievement in Russia

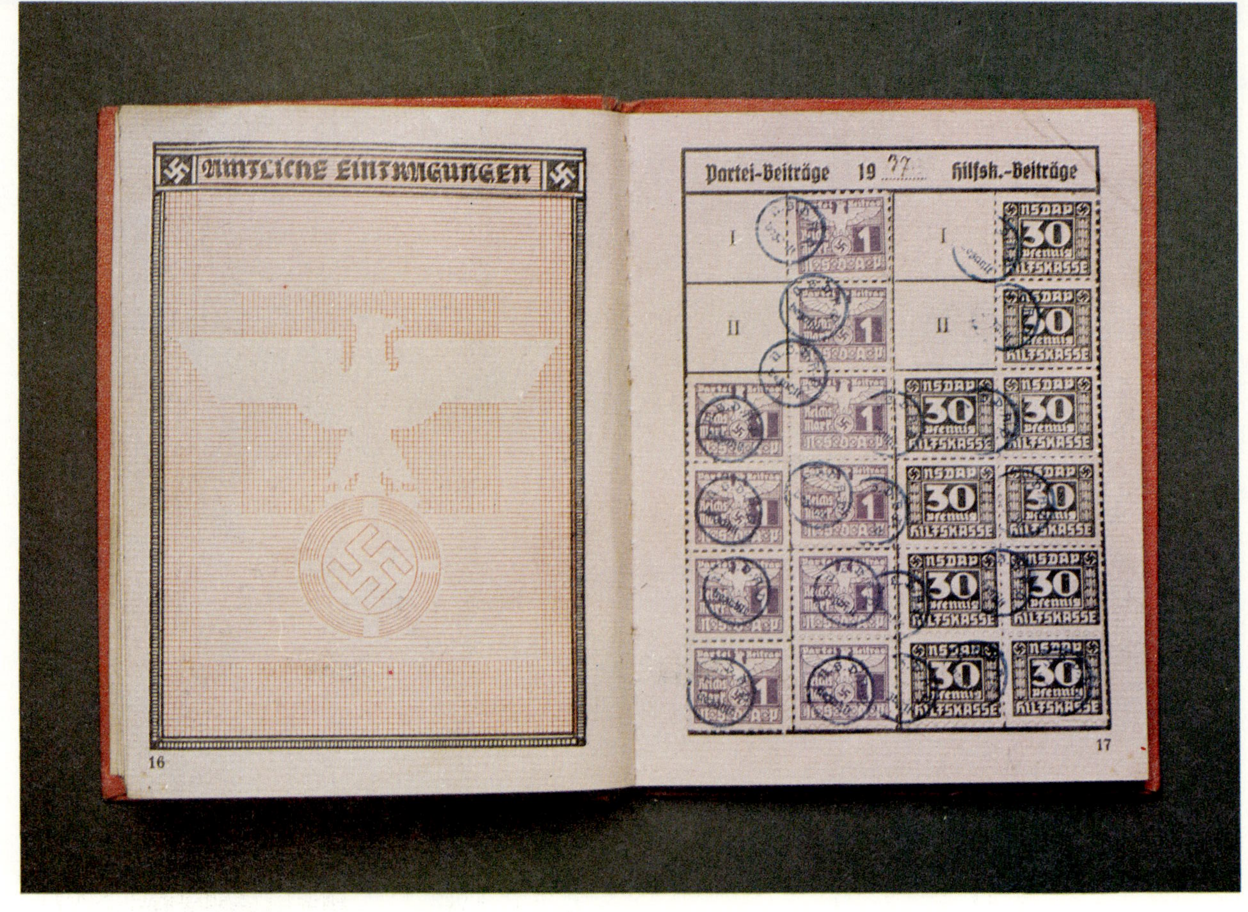

Page showing contribution stamps in Kurt Meyer's membership book shown on opposite page

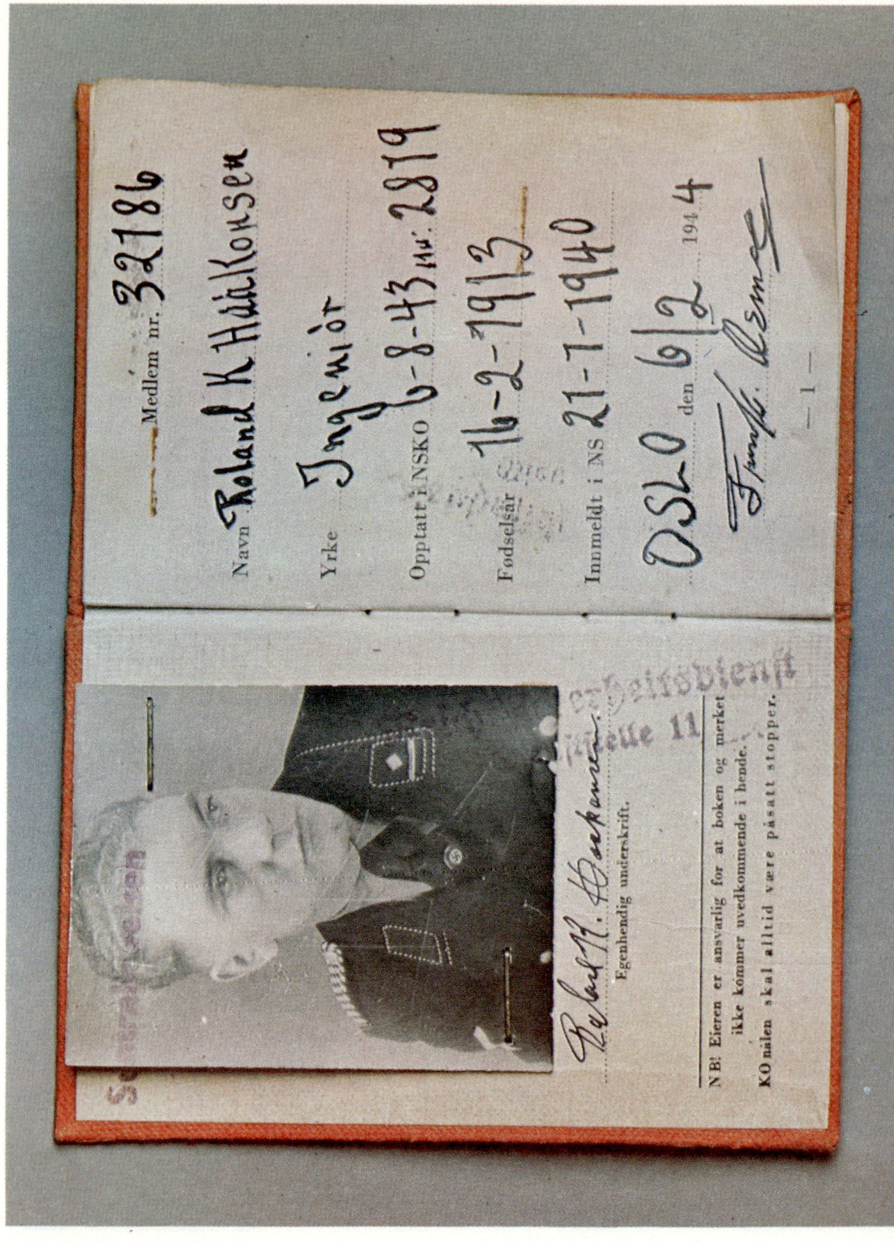

Germanisches membership book of the Nasjonal Samling (Norwegian Nazi Party). This example was issued to an SS-NCO and bears the stamp of the SS Security Department

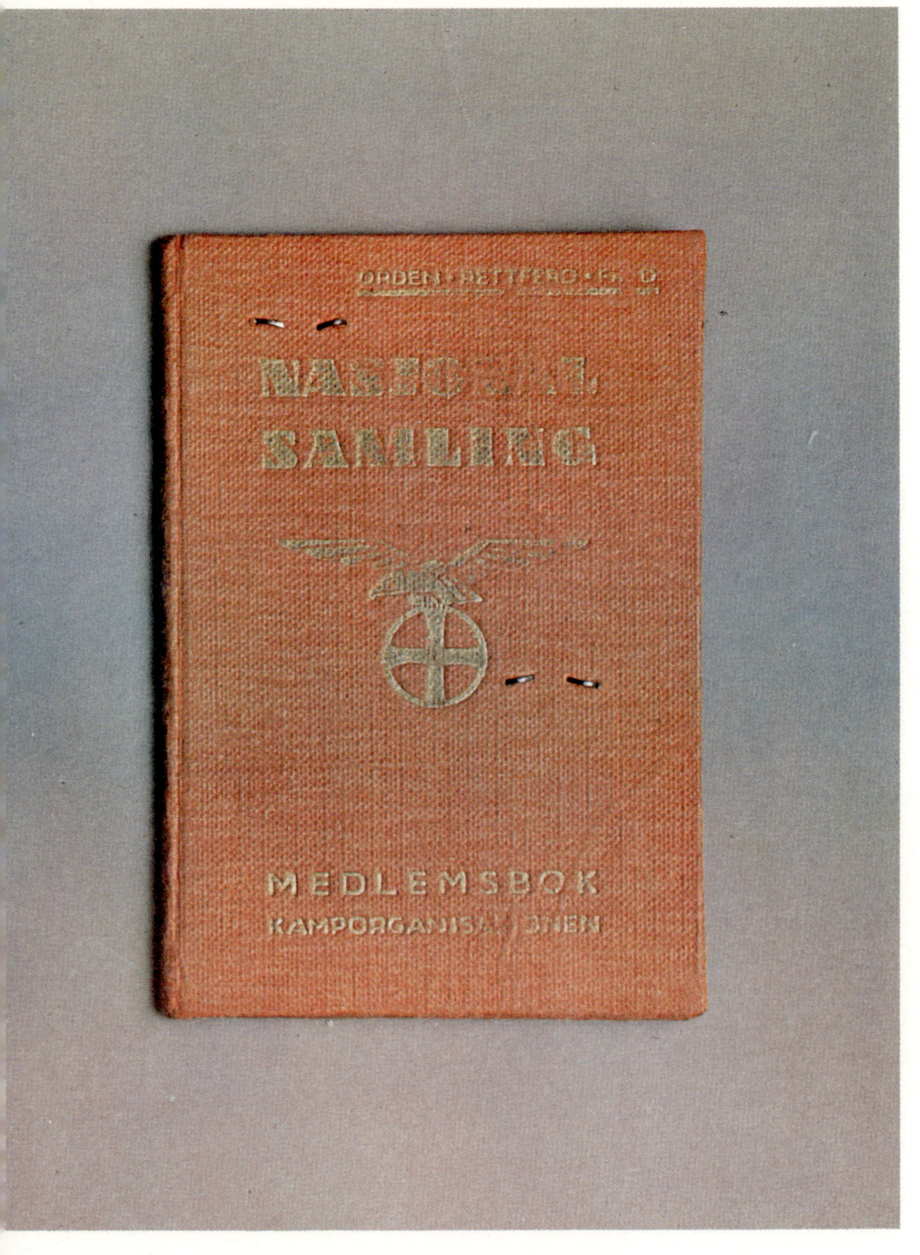

Cover of the book, shown on opposite page, distinctive eagle of Norwegian Nazi Party.

SS shield taken from wall of SS barracks at the rear of Schönbrunn Palace, Vienna

Wreath band. These were attached to wreaths sent by local SS leaders to the funerals of fallen SS men. This example is from the SS leader in the Flanders district

SS Untersturmführer wearing the old style Feldmütze and with the grass pattern camouflage smock rolled up for comfort and worn over the field-service tunic and service breeches with officers high boots. Around his neck are hung binoculars and he is holding a M P 40

SS Hauptsturmführer from the Leibstandarte SS 'Adolf Hitler' Panzer Division and Knights Cross Holder wearing a short cross over black Panzer uniform with trousers gathered at the ankles and short black boots. Head-dress is the officers Feldmütze. Map case and pistol holsters are shown

SS Unterscharführer wearing the field grey uniform for self-propelled artillery gun crews. Steel helmet and canvas gaiters over short boots complete the outfit. Decorations shown are Iron Cross 1st Class and Iron Cross 2nd Class ribbon

SS Hauptscharführer from the SS Totenkopf Division wearing 'autumn' pattern camouflage smock and helmet cover. Trousers tucked into marching boots. Rifle ammo pouches are supported by a set of black leather 'Y' straps. A water bottle is hung from the belt and entrenching tool just visible

Waffen SS rank insignia

Top left: Generaloberst der Waffen SS. *Second row left:* General der Waffen SS. *Third row left:* Generalleutnant der Waffen SS. *Bottom left:* Generalmajor der Waffen SS. *Top right:* SS Oberführer. *Second row right:* SS Standartenführer. *Third row right:* Obersturmbannführer. *Bottom right:* SS Sturmbannführer

op left: SS Hauptsturmbannführer. Second row left: SS Obersturmführer. Third row left: SS Untersturmführer.
ottom row left: SS Sturmscharführer. Top right: Hauptscharführer. Second row right: Oberscharführer. Third row
ight: Scharführer. Bottom row right: Unterscharführer

SS Brigadeführer und Generalmajor der Waffen SS, Kurt Meyer 'Panzermeyer' Holder of the Knights Cross with oakleaves and swords.

Sepp. Dietrich, Commander of the SS Liebstandarte 'Adolf Hitler' in Winter uniform wearing the Knights Cross with Oakleaves.

Decorations

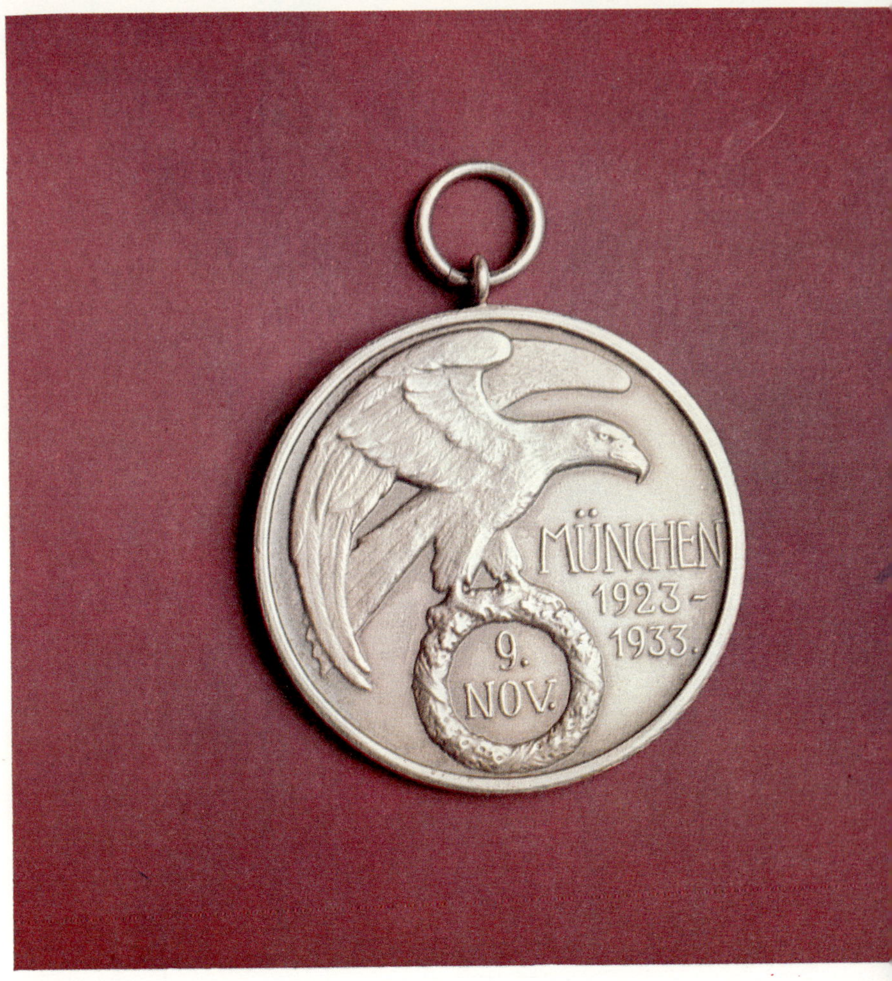

Blutorden (Blood Order): originally Ehrenzeichen vom 9th November 1923, instituted in March 1934 and awarded to participants of the 'Putsch' (the rebellion against the Munich government). Renamed Blutorden and given as party decoration for outstanding merit until 1942, some posthumously awarded. This order was worn with red, white and black ribbon on right breast pocket

verse of opposite page.

Top: Deutsches Reiterabzeichen. Instituted on 9th April 1930 in three grades, and awarded for 'outstanding achievement in the field of equestrian sport'. *Bottom:* Deutsches Fahrerabzeichen. Instituted May 1930 in three grades, and awarded for 'outstanding achievement in the horse driving branch of equestrian sport'.

Top: Heeres-Flakabzeichen (Army Anti-aircraft Badge) 18th July 1941. At first for shooting down five aircraft but from July 1943 awarded on a points system – 2 points for each aircraft, a total of 16 points for the award.
Bottom: Kraftfahrbewahrungsabzeichen (Motor Transport Driver's Award) 23rd October 1942. For drivers who distinguished themselves while driving in difficult conditions in certain eastern, northern and African theatres of war for a given number of operational days. It was issued in three grades: gold, silver and bronze. The badge could be forfeited for neglect of vehicle, exceeding the speed limit or causing an accident.

Left: Medaille zur Erinnerung an die Heimkehr des Memel Landes (Commemorative medal for the return of the Memel). Instituted on 1st May 1939 for 'Merit during the return of the Memel area to the German Reich'.
Centre: Medaille Zur Erinnerung an den 13 März 1938 (Commemorative Medal of the 13th March 1938). Instituted on 1st May 1938 for merit during the Union of Austria and the Third Reich and awarded to all participants. This the first of the so-called Blumenfeldzugsmedaillen (flower campaign medals). *Right:* Medaille Zur Erinnerung 1st October 1938 (Commemorative Medal of 1st October 1938). Instituted on 18th October 1938 for merit during the reunion of the Sudeten-German areas with the German Reich and awarded to all participants.

Reverse of opposite page.

Nahkampfspange Close-Combat Clasp 25th November 1942.
Top: Gold for 50 hand-to-hand actions. *Centre:* Silver for 30 hand-to-hand actions. *Bottom:* Bronze for 15 hand-to-hand actions.
Worn above breast pocket

Verwundetenabzeichen 1939. The wound badge was revived by an Order of 22nd May 1939 for German personnel wounded in the Spanish Civil War 1936–1939. Similar to that of 1914–1918 but with a swastika added to the steel helmet. It was issued only in black (182) and silver (1). An order of 1st September 1939 restored the three grades of black, silver and gold as in the First World War. Both were worn on the left breast without ribbon as in the First World War.

Medaille 'Winterschlacht im Osten 1941–42'. Front and reverse (Medal of Winter Battle in the East 1941–42), instituted on 26th May 1942 for all military and non-military formations which between 15th November and 15th April 1942 had served at the Eastern front for at least fourteen days in the case of combatants, or sixty days for non-combatants. The zone of the award was Ukraine, Ostland or the operational area Finland eastwards of the Finnish-Russian border of 1940. This so called 'Gefrierfleischorden' (Frozen Meat Order) is a dark coloured iron medal worn from a red ribbon with one black stripe in the middle, worn on the Ordensschnalle, or with the field uniform the ribbon could be worn in the buttonhole.

SS Dienstauszeichnung (SS Long Service Award) instituted 30th January 1938 and issued in four grades.
Left: Stufe for 25 years (war years and the period 1925 to 1933 counted double) — gilt swastika with wording 'Für Treue Dienste in der SS' on the reverse. Worn from a cornflower blue ribbon with golden embroidery; Feldschnalle ribbon decorated with gilt 'runes'. *Right:* Stufe for 12 years — silver coloured swastika, wording as above on reverse, blue ribbon with silver embroidery, silver coloured 'runes' on the Feldschnalle ribbon.

Left: Spange 1939 Zum EKI (Bar 1939 for EK 1st Class). Both cross and bar were instituted on 1st September 1939. The silver coloured bar was issued for those who already owned the Iron Cross 1st Class 1914 and again was awarded with the same decoration. The pin back bar was worn above the Iron Cross 1st Class 1914. *Top:* Ritterkreuz Des Eiseren Kreuzesdmit dem Eichenlaub mit Schwerten (Knight's Cross with Oak leaves with swords), instituted on 21st June 1941. This is a neck decoration. *Right:* Bar to Iron Cross 2nd Class, usually worn on the ribbon of the 1915 cross. *Bottom:* Eisernes Kreuz I Klasse – (Iron Cross 1st Class) – silver edged, black cross, worn on the left breast.

Top: Ritterkreuz des KVK (Knight's Cross of the War Merit Cross) a neck decoration instituted on 8th July 1944, which could be awarded with and without swords. The date '1939' is shown on the reverse of the award.
Right: Kriegsverdienstkreuz 2 Klasse – KVK II (War Merit Cross 2nd Class) a bronze metal ribbon decoration awarded with or without swords and worn on the left breast. The ribbon of the Feldschnalle (undress ribbons) could be worn with or without the addition of the swords. *Left:* Kriegsverdienstkreuz I Klasse (War Merit Cross 1st Class) a silver covered metal pinback cross, awarded with or without swords and worn on the left breast.
Bottom: Kreigsverdienstmedaille (War Merit Medal) a bronze metal decoration with the wording 'Für Kriegsverdienst 1939' in gothic lettering on the reverse. The ribbon is that of the KVK II but with the addition of a red stripe in the middle. The medal could be awarded without swords only.

Left: Ehrenblatt-Spange Des Heeres (Honour Roll Clasp, Army) March 1944. For citation in Order of the Day (Tagesbefehl). Ribbon worn attached to tunic buttonhole. *Right:* Iron Cross 2nd Class. Instituted in 1939. On the first day of award it was worn in the second button hole and after that the ribbon only was worn. In full dress the cross was worn above the breast pocket suspended from its ribbon.

Sturmabzeichen Assault Badge for troops supporting infantry or tank assaults, awarded for three assaults. After July 1943 further grades were issued for 25, 50, 75 and 100 engagements.

Above: Fallschirmschützenabzeichen (Airforce parachutist's Badge) 5th November 1936. *Below:* Fallschirmschützenabzeichen (Army parachutist's Badge) 1st September 1937. For at least six jumps in one year and subject to annual renewal. Superseded by the Luftwaffe parachutist's Award.

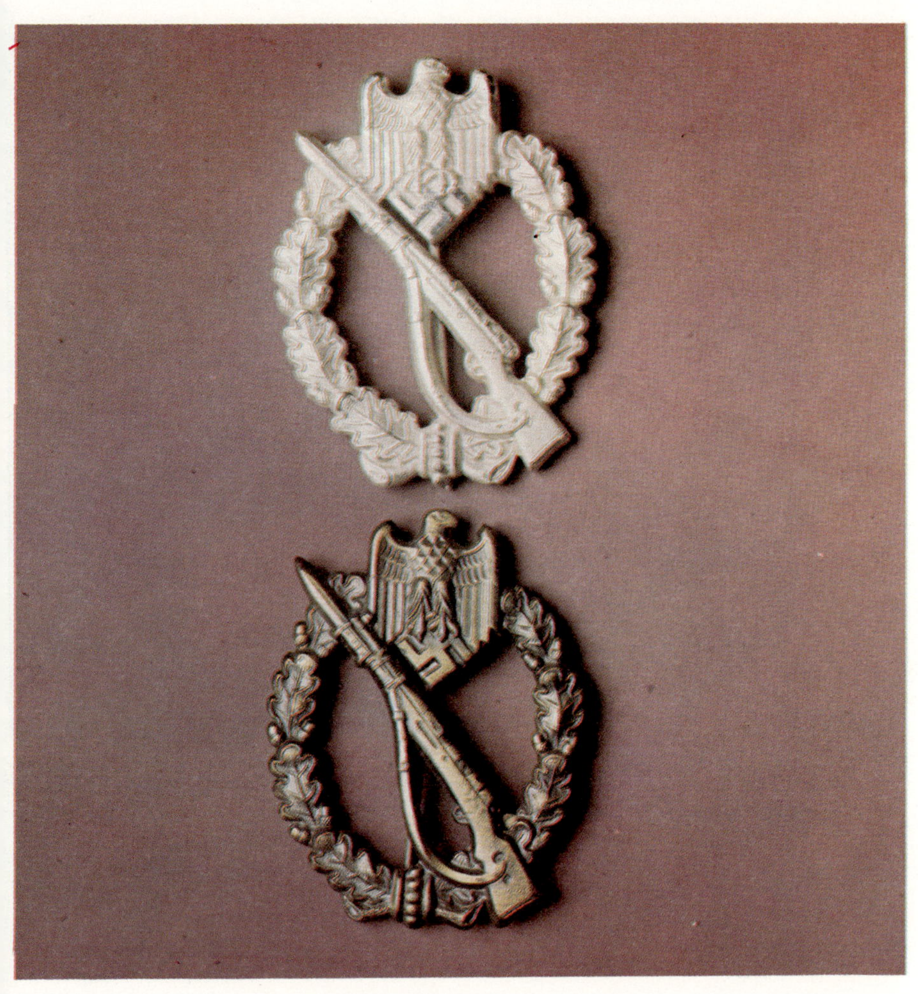

Infanterie-Sturmabzeichen (Infantry Assault Badge) 20th December 1939, awarded for three assault operations.
Silver for rifle and mountain infantry companies, bronze for motorised infantry units.

Panzerkampfabzeichen (Tank Engagement Badge), 20th December 1939. Silver for Panzer units, bronze for Panzer Grenadier Regiments, motorcycle battalians of Panzer divisions and tank reconnaissance personnel. After July 1943 further grades were issued for 20, 50, 75 and 100 engagements.

Badge issued for SA meeting at Braunschweig, 17th–18th October 1931. This rally developed into a street battle with the Communists, resulting in many of the SA and SS being killed. As a result this badge became a decoration.

Top left: Krimschild (Crimea Campaign Badge) instituted on 25th July 1942 by Adolf Hitler 'in memory of the heroic battles at the Krim'. The Krimschild in gold was given to the German Generalfeldmarschall von Manstein and the Rumanian Marshal Antonescu. *Top right:* Kubanschild (Kuban Campaign badge) instituted on 20th September 1943 by Adolf Hitler 'in memory of the months of heroic defence in the battle area of Kuban against overwhelming forces'. *Bottom:* Cholmschild (Cholm Campaign Badge) instituted on 1st July 1942 by Adolf Hitler 'in memory of the months of heroic defence of Cholm against the numerically heavier enemy forces'. Cholm is in Russia in the neighbourhood of Novgorod near the Lavat river.

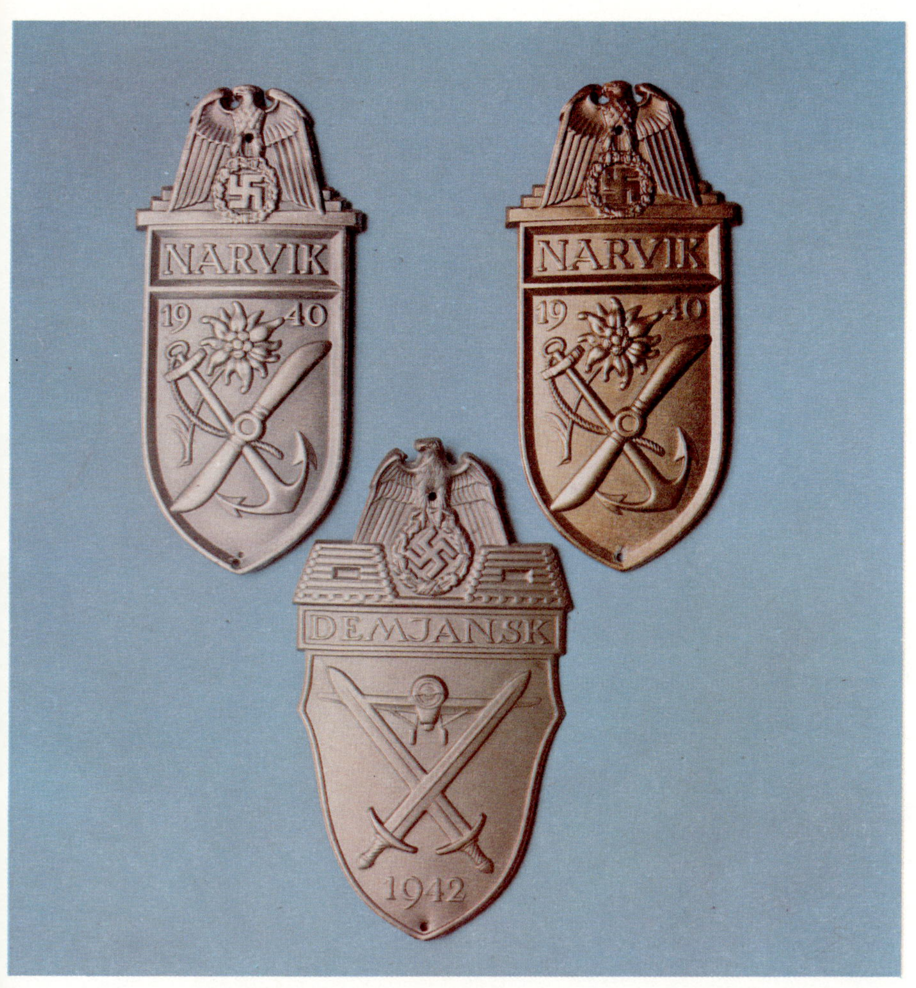

Top left and right: Narvikschild (Narvik Campaign Badge) instituted on 19th August 1940 by Adolf Hitler for members of Heer, Kriegsmarine and Luftwaffe who took part in the landings in Narvik (Norway) or battles of the Group Narvik. Members of Heer and Luftwaffe received a silver coloured badge and members of Kriegsmarine a gilt coloured badge.
Bottom: Demjanskschild (Demjansk Campaign Badge), instituted on 25th April 1943 by Adolf Hitler 'in memory of the months of heroic defence in the battle area of Demjansk (Russia, near Novgorod) against overwhelming forces'

SS long-service medals. *Left:* SS four-year long-service medal, reverse. *Right:* obverse of the same medal in case of issue

Long-service medal reverse. *Left:* Eight-year. *Right:* obverse of the same medal

Tapferkeits – und Verdienst – Auszeichnung für Angehörige der Ostvokan (decoration for Bravery and Merit of the 'Eastern People').

Hoping to free themselves and their homeland from the pressure of Bolshevism, thousands of Russians joined the foreign auxiliary forces to fight for Germany in other countries. For members of this legion a decoration was instituted on 14th July 1942 as a visible sign of appreciation for bravery and merit. Although the decoration, according to the conditions of award, was meant for 'East Folk' volunteers only, it was also awarded to Germans. Two versions of this award exist: for 'bravery', symbolized by a star with swords; and for 'merit', without swords. Both versions had two classes and five grades

(a) Klasse in gold – gilt star with green and red ribbon, worn from the Ordensschnalle.

(b) Klasse in silber – silver coloured star with green and white ribbon.

(c) Klasse in bronze – bronze coloured star with plain green ribbon.

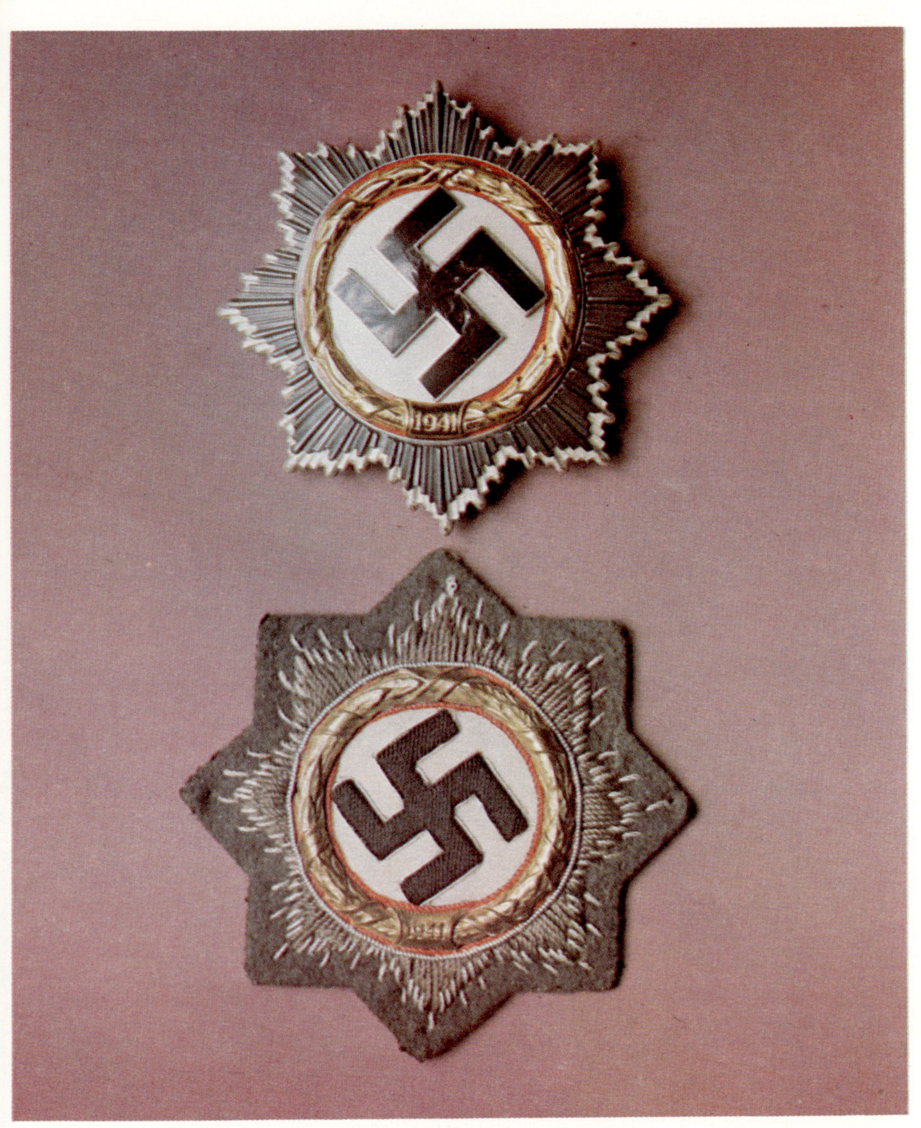

Deutsches Kreuz (German Cross), instituted on 28th September 1941 as 'Kriegsorden des Deutschen Kreuzes' (War Order of the German Cross) awarded as appreciation for many extraordinary deeds of courage and leadership. The only German award for individual acts of bravery. There were two classes – gold and silver – which was shown by the colour of wreath around the the swastika. There are two versions, cloth and metal. The cloth version is produced in airforce blue, field grey and navy blue, although intended for respective coloured uniform they were frequently mixed up

Typical group of medals as worn by the SS. *Left to right:* Iron Cross 2nd Class 1914–1918: War Merit Cross 2nd Class without swords: Cross of Honour of the 1914–18 war: Westwall medal: SS four-year long-service medal

Top: Collar patch of the SS Fliegersturm. *Bottom:* Pilots wings of the SS Fliegersturm

Security Services

Top: Pair of collar patches worn by SS Sturmbannführer in the security service of the SS. *Centre:* Collar patches worn by SS Oberscharführer in the security service of the SS; piping was discontinued in 1942. *Bottom left:* Sleeve diamond worn on lower left sleeve by officers of the security service of the SS (SD) who transferred from the Gestapo when it was incorporated into the security service of the SS in 1936. *Bottom centre:* Shoulder strap worn by SS Oberschaführrer of the security service of the SS 1942–1945. *Bottom right:* Sleeve diamond worn by all non-commissioned members of the security service of the SS on the lower left sleeve

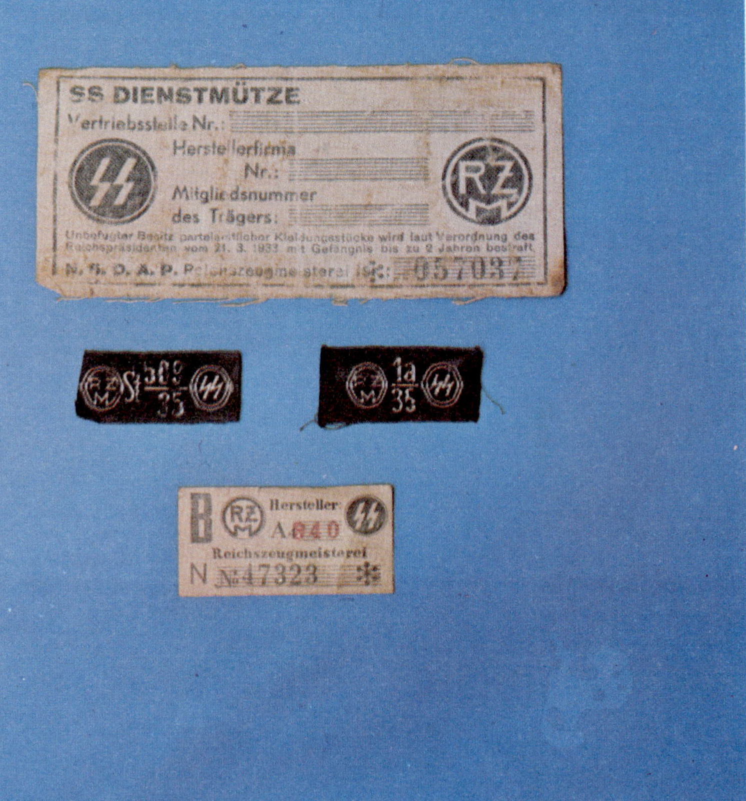

Top: RZM Control label from an SS issue service cap. *Centre:* RZM Control label, cloth version found on pre-war SS insignia. *Bottom:* Control label, paper version found on wartime SS insignia

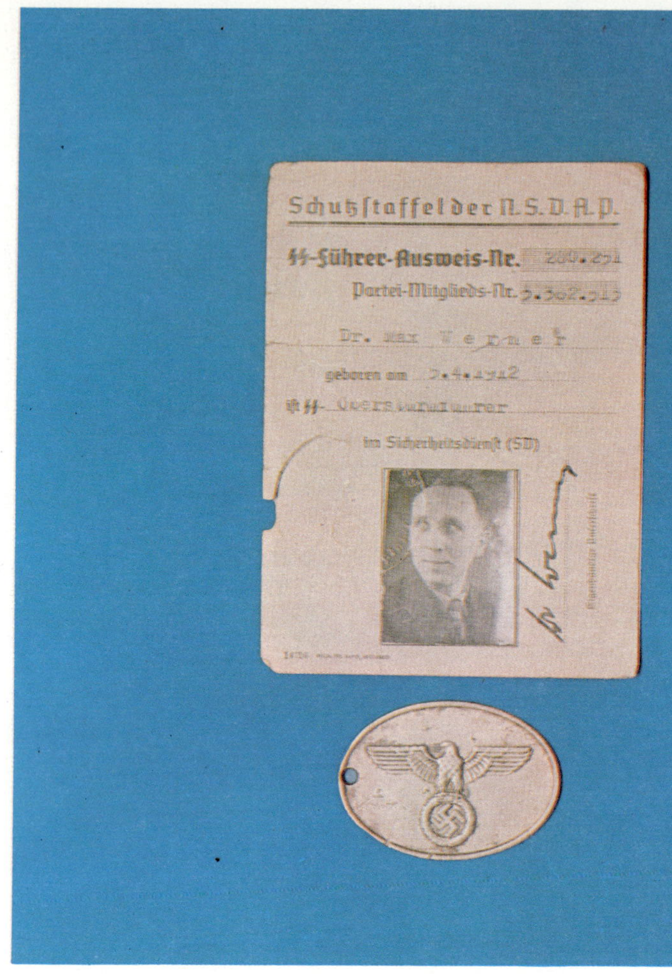

Top: SS officer's identification card, carried by an SS Obersturmführer in the SD (Sicherheitsdienst – Security Service of the SS). *Bottom:* Gestapo (Geheime Staatspolizei – Secret State Police) warrant disc

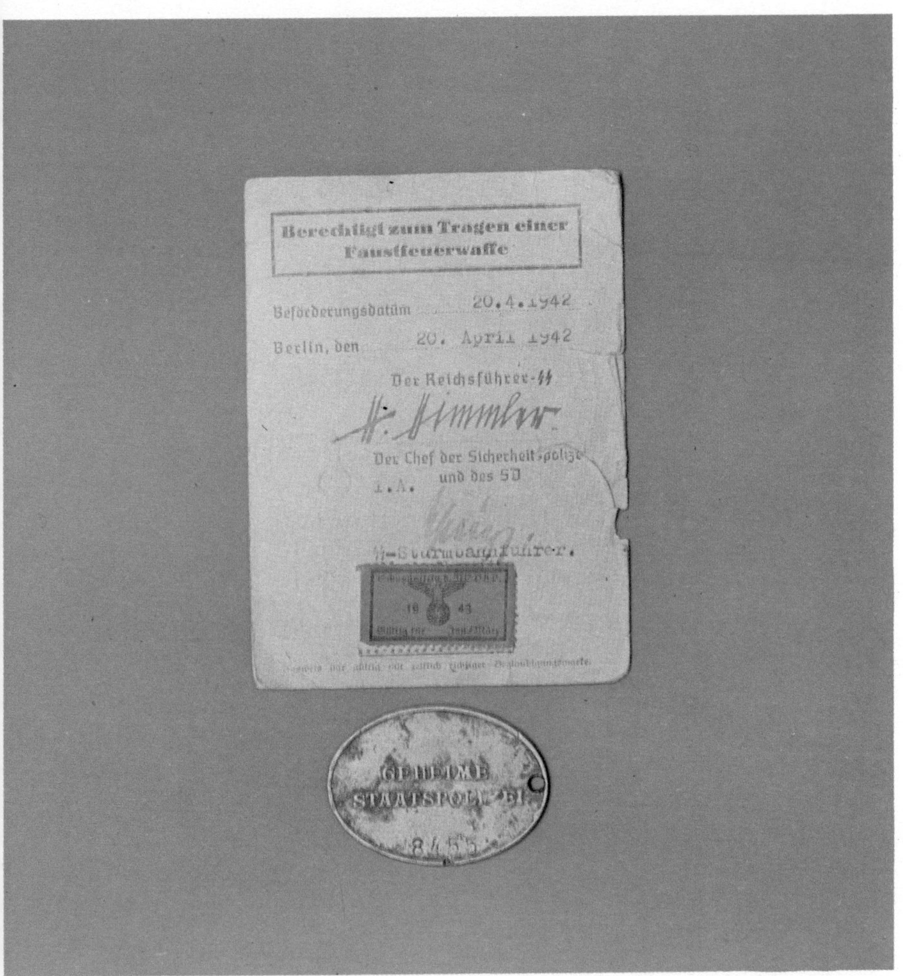

Reverse of opposite page

Top: Armband worn by Security Police Auxiliaries. *Bottom left:* Badge worn by SS police on the field cap. *Bottom centre:* Arm badge worn by Auxiliary Security Police personnel (Schutzmannschaften). *Bottom right:* Badge worn by Schutzmannschaften on the field cap

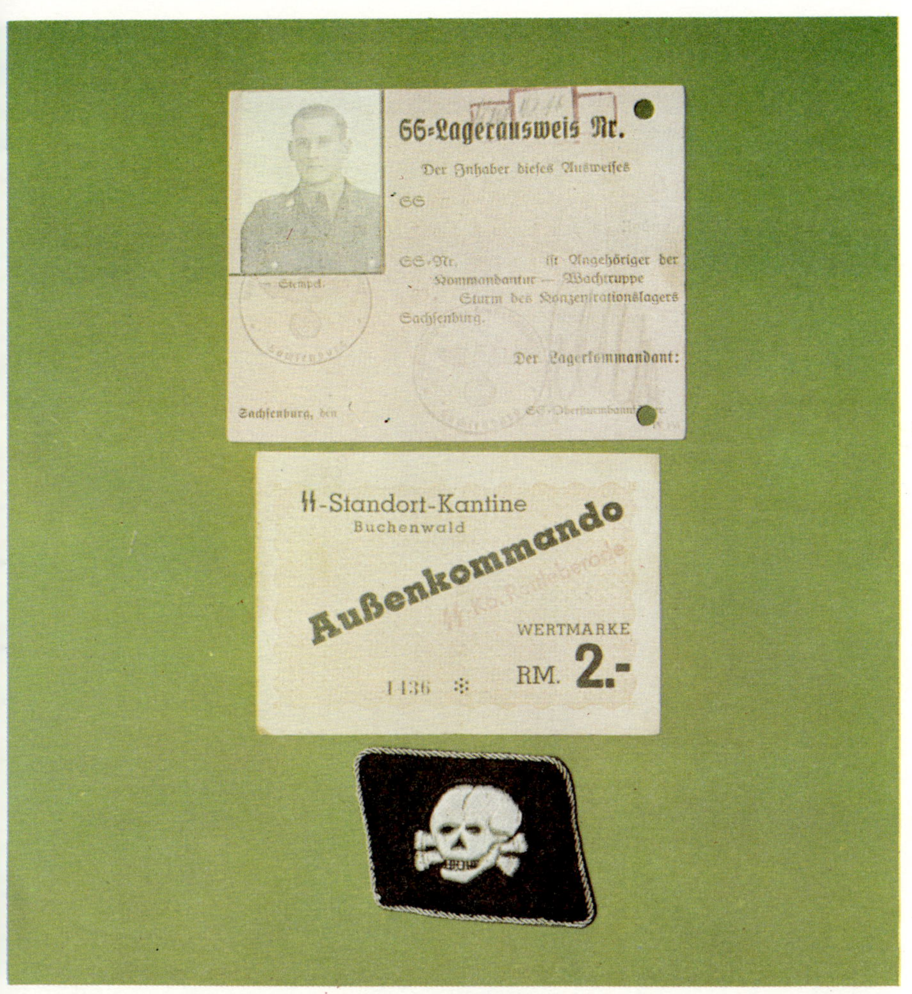

Top: SS concentration camp guard's pass from Sachsenburg. *Centre:* Two Reichsmark note from Buchenwald concentration camp. *Bottom:* Collar patch worn by commissioned officers on concentration camp units and the Waffen SS Death's Head units

Der Reichsführer SS
Adjutantur

73/43 J. Adler

Reichssicherheitshauptamt
Nachrichten-Uebermittlung

Aufgenommen				Raum für Eingangsstempel	Befördert			
Zeit	Tag	Monat	Jahr		Zeit	Tag	Monat	Jahr
von		durch		1943	an		durch	

N.-Ü. Nr.

Telegramm — Funkspruch — Fernschreiben
Fernspruch

Geh. Kdo.-Sache!

BLITZ GKDOS PERS. STAB RFSS BERLIN NR.

1246 9.3.43 1900 = DIE = = = =

AN DEN REICHSFUEHRER - SS UND CHEF DER

DEUTSCHEN POLIZEI FELD-KOMMANDOSTELLE = = = =

VS- TGB. NR. 173 /43 G. KDOS. =

C. ADJ. VS - TGB. NR. 91 /43 G. KDOS. =

REICHSFUEHRER = = = =

1.) DIE VERHANDLUNGEN WEGEN DER BOSNIAKEN- DIVISION

SIND ABGESCHLOSSEN. BEIDERSEITIGE UEBEREINSTIMMUNG

WURDE ERZIELT. DIE KROATISCHE REGIERUNG GLAUBT

ALLERDINGS, VOR DURCHFUEHRUNG DER BETROFFENEN

VEREINBARUNG NOCH DIE GENEHMIGUNG DER ITALIENISCHEN

REGIERUNG EINHOLEN ZU MUESSEN. = =

G.St. Nr. 120.

Telegram from security service of SS to Heinrich Himmler (continued on reverse side) initialled in top right corner by Himmler, who often used green pencil

All Nazi party insignia was marked by the RZM (Reichszeugmeisterei – National Ordnance Department). *Blue label:* SA party items here shown on SA armband. *Black label:* SS items here shown on SS shoulder strap. *Red label:* Hitler Youth items here shown on cloth version of Hitler Youth proficiency badge. *Black embroidered label:* Early SS items here shown on SS armband (this is reverse side of armbands on page 31 Allegemeine SS section)

Army style tunic, field grey parade dress, about 1942. Reichssicherheitshaupamt. (Main Security Department of the SS, founded in 1939 with the amalgamation of all the various branches of the security service.)

SS Hauptsturmführer Reichssicherheitshauptamt (main security department of the SS). This pattern of field grey uniform is identical to the black uniform and was introduced in 1938. It was normally worn with aiguillette in parade dress. The brocade belt was introduced in 1938

BADGES OF THE SCHUTZSTAFFELN DIVISIONS

1   I SS Panzer Division 'Leibstandarte'
2   II SS Panzer Division 'Das Reich'
3   III SS Panzer Division 'Totenkopf'
4   IV SS Pz Gren Division 'Polizei Division'
5   V SS Panzer Division 'Wiking'
6   VI SS Mountain Division 'Nord'
7   VII SS Vol Mnt Division 'Prinz Eugen'
8   VIII SS Cavalry Division 'Florian Geyer'
9   IX SS Panzer Division 'Hohenstaufen'
10   X SS Panzer Division 'Frundsberg'

11   XI SS Frw Pz Gren Division 'Nordland'
12   XII SS Panzer Division 'Hitlerjugend'
13   XIII SS Mountain Division 'Handschar'
14   XIV SS Waffen Gren Division 'Galizische No I'
15   XV SS Waffen Gren Division 'Latvian No I'
16   XVI SS Pz Gren Division 'Reichsführer SS'
17   XVII SS Pz Gren Division 'Gotz von Berlichingen'
18   XVIII SS Vol Pz Gren Division 'Horst Wessel'
19   XIX SS Waffen Gren Division 'Latvian No II'
20   XX SS Waffen Gren Division 'Estonian No I'

21	XXI Waffen Geb Div der SS 'Skanderbeg'
22	XXII SS Frw Kav Division 'Maria Theresa'
23	XXIII SS Vol Pz Gren Division 'Nederland'
24	XXIV SS Waffen Mountain Div 'Karstjäger'
25	XXV SS Waffen Gren Division 'Hungarian No II'
26	XXVI SS Waffen Gren Division 'Hungarian No III'
27	XXVII SS Vol Gren Division 'Flemish No I'
28	XXVIII SS Vol Pz Gren Division 'Wallonie'
29	XXIX SS Waffen Gren Division 'Italian No I'
30	XXX SS Waffen Gren Division 'Russian No II'
31	XXXI SS Frw Gren Division
32	SS Frw Gren Division 'Böhmen-Mähren'
33	XXXII SS Vol Gren Division 'January 30'
34	XXXIII SS Waffen Gren Division 'Charlemagne'
35	XXXIV SS Gren Division 'Landstorm Nederland'
36	XXXV SS Pol Gren Division 'Polizei Division II'
37	XXXVI SS Waffen Gren Division 'Dirlewanger'
38	XXXVII SS Vol Cavalry Division 'Lützow'
39	XXXVIII SS Pz Gren Division 'Nibelungen'

Battle Order of the Waffen ⚡⚡ divisions

The style conferred on the Waffen SS divisions varied, depending on its racial composition. Those composed of German volunteers were styled 'SS-Division'; those of 'racial' Germans or Germanic volunteers, 'SS-Freiwilligen-Division'; those of east Europeans, 'Division der Waffen SS'. In all cases the number (conferred in 1942) came first and the name last; where necessary, a national description was appended.

Name	Raised	Composition	Strength	Fate
1st SS Panzerdivision Leibstandarte Adolf Hitler	1933	German	successively a regiment, brigade and division	Capitulated 1945
2nd SS Panzerdivision Das Reich	1939	German	divisional	Capitulated 1945
3rd SS Panzerdivision Totenkopf	1940	German	divisional	Capitulated 1945
4th SS Polizei-Panzergrenadierdivision	1940	German	divisional	Capitulated 1945
5th SS Panzerdivision Wiking	late 1940	German/West European	divisional	Capitulated 1945
6th SS Gebirgsdivision Nord	late 1940	German	brigade, later divisional	Capitulated 1945
7th SS Freiwilligen-Gebirgsdivision Prinz Eugen	1942	Racial German from Yugoslavia	divisional	Capitulated 1945

8th SS Kavalleriedivision Florian Geyer	1942	German/racial German	divisional	Capitulated 1945
9th SS Panzerdivision Hohenstauffen	1943	German	divisional	Capitulated 1945
10th SS Panzerdivision Frundsberg	1943	German	divisional	Capitulated 1945
11th SS Freiwilligen-Panzergrenadierdivision Nordland	late 1942	German/West European	divisional	Capitulated 1945
12th SS Panzerdivision Hitler Jugend	1943	German	divisional	Capitulated 1945
13th Waffen-Gebirgsdivision der SS Handschar (Kroatische Nr 1)	1943	Yugoslav Muslim	divisional	Disbanded 1944
14th Waffen-Grenadier-division der SS (Galizische Nr 1)	1943	Ukranian	divisional	Capitulated 1945
15th Waffen-Grenadier-division der SS (Lettische Nr 1)	1943	Latvian/ German	divisional	Capitulated 1945
16th SS Panzergrenadier-division Reichsführer SS	1943	German/racial German	divisional	Capitulated 1945
17th SS Panzergrenadier-division Götz von Berlichingen	1943	German/racial German	divisional	Capitulated 1945
18th SS Freiwilligen-Panzergrenadierdivision Horst Wessel	1944	German/racial German	divisional	Capitulated 1945
19th Waffen Grenadier-division der SS (Lettische Nr 2)	1944	Latvian	divisional	Capitulated 1945
20th Waffen Grenadier-division der SS (Estnische Nr 1)	1944	Estonian	divisional	Capitulated 1945

21st Waffen Gebirgsdivision der SS Skanderberg (Albanische Nr 1)	1944	Albanian Muslim	never fully formed	Disbanded 1944
22nd SS Freiwilligen-Kavalleriedivision Maria Theresia	1944	Racial German/ German	divisional	Capitulated 1945
23rd Waffen Gebirgsdivision der SS Kama (Kroatische Nr 2)	1944	Yugoslav Muslim	never fully formed	Disbanded 1944
(2) 23rd SS Freiwilligen-Panzerdivision Nederland	1945	Dutch	regimental	Capitulated 1945
24th Waffen Gebirgskarst jägerdivision der SS	1944	Italian/racial German	unknown	Dissolved 1945
25th Waffen Grenadier-division der SS Hunyadi (Ungarische Nr 1)	late 1944	Hungarian	unknown	Disappeared
26th Waffen Grenadier-division der SS (Ungarische Nr 2)	late 1944	Hungarian	unknown	Disappeared
27th SS Freiwilligen-Grenadierdivision Langemarck	1945	Flemish-Belgian	regimental	Capitulated 1945
28th SS Freiwilligen-Grenadierdivision Wallonien	1945	Walloon-Belgian	regimental	Capitulated 1945
29th Waffen Grenadier-division der SS (Russische Nr 1)	1944	Russian	regimental	Transferred to the Vlasov Army 1944
(2) 29th Waffen Grenadier-division der SS (Italienische Nr 1)	1945	Italian	regimental	Disappeared 1945
30th Waffen Grenadier-division der SS (Russische Nr 2)	1944	Russian	regimental	Transferred to the Vlasov Army 1944

31st SS Freiwilligen-Panzerdivision Böhmen-Mähren	1945	German/ racial German	regimental	Capitulated 1945
32nd SS Panzergrenadier-division 30 Januar	1945	German	regimental	Capitulated 1945
33rd Waffen Kavallerie-division der SS (Ungarische Nr 3)	1945	Hungarian	regimental	Annihilated 1945
(2) 33rd Waffen Grenadier-division der SS Charlemagne (Französische Nr 1)	1945	French	regimental	Annihilated Berlin 1945
34th SS Freiwilligen-Grenadierdivision Landstorm Nederland	1945	Dutch	regimental	Dissolved 1945
35th SS Polizei-Grenadierdivision	1945	German Policemen	regimental	Dissolved 1945
36th Waffen Grenadier-division der SS	1945	Originally Dirlewanger's Brigade	brigade	Capitulated 1945
37th SS Freiwilligen-Kavalleriedivision Lützow	1945	Racial German	regimental	Capitulated 1945
38th Panzergrenadier-division Nibelungen	1945	SS Officer cadets	regimental	Capitulated 1945

Notes:
1. 23rd (2), 27th, 28th and 33rd (2) were originally 'Legions', belonging either to the SS or the army.
2. Most units numbered above 20 were of indifferent quality or under-strength.
3. Gebirgsdivision: mountain division; Grenadierdivision: infantry division; Panzer-grenadierdivision: motorised infantry division.

Table of equivalent ranks

British/U.S. Army	SS	German Army	Waffen-SS
Field-Marshal US General of Army	Reichsführer	Generalfeldmarschall	Reichsführer-SS
No equivalent	Oberstgruppenführer (from 1942 only)	Generaloberst	SS-Oberstgruppenführer und Generaloberst der Waffen-SS
General	Obergruppenführer	General der Infanterie	SS-Obergruppenführer und General der Waffen-SS
Lieutenant-General	Gruppenführer	Generalleutnant	SS-Gruppenführer und Generalleutnant der Waffen-SS
Major-General	Brigadeführer	Generalmajor	SS Brigadeführer und Generalmajor der Waffen-SS
Brigadier US Brigadier-General	Oberführer	Oberst	SS-Oberführer
Colonel	Standartenführer	Oberst	SS-Standartenführer

Lieutenant-Colonel	Obersturmbannführer	Oberstleutnant	SS-Obersturmbannführer
Major	Sturmbannführer	Major	Sturmbannführer
Captain	Hauptsturmführer	Hauptmann, Rittmeister	SS-Hauptsturmführer
Lieutenant US 1st Lieutenant	Obersturmführer	Oberleutnant	SS-Obersturmführer
Second Lieutenant	Untersturmführer	Leutnant	SS-Untersturmführer
Regimental Sergeant-Major US Sergeant-Major	Sturmscharführer	Hauptfeldwebel	SS-Sturmscharführer
Sergeant-Major US Master-Sergeant	Hauptscharführer	Oberfahnriche, Oberfeldwebel	Hauptscharführer
Staff Sergeant	Scharführer	Fahnriche, Unterfeldwebel	SS-Standartenjunker, Scharführer
Sergeant	Unterscharführer	Unteroffizier, Oberjäger	SS-Unterscharführer
Corporal	Rottenführer	Obergefreiter	SS-Rottenführer
Lance-Corporal US Private 1st Class	Sturmmann	Oberschutze	SS-Oberschutze
Private	SS-Mann	Schutze	SS-Schutze

Glossary of terms

Abschnitt
Regional subdivision of the territorial organisation of the SS. Also regional HQ of the SD

Abt Landesverteidigung
The National Defence Branch in the OKW

Abteilung
A branch, section or subdivision of a main department or office. Also a military unit or detachment up to battalion strength

Abwehrpolizei
Counter espionage police, part of the Grenzpolizei controlled by the Gestapo

Abzeichen
Appointment, Badge of Rank or distinction

Ahnenerbe Forschungs und Lehrgemeischaft
Society for research into and Teaching of Ancestral Heritage. It promoted the study and teaching of Nazi racial theories ; administered by the SS

Allgemeine SS
The main body of the SS composed of full and part time, inactive and honorary members. Distinct from the Waffen SS

Amt
Main office or directorate of a ministry

Amt VI
Foreign intelligence service of the SD

Amtsgericht
Law court

Amtsgruppe
Branch of an Hauptamt

Anhaltelager
Temporary detention camp

Anordnung
A regulation or an order

Anwarter
SS cadet or candidate

Arbeitseinsatzführer
Chief supervisor of labour in a concentration camp

Aufklärung
Military Reconnaissance

Ausbildung
Training

Auslands Organisation
NSDAP agency for the supervision of Germans living abroad. Ranked as a Gaue

Aussendienststelle
Outpost of the Sipo and SD

Aussenkommando
A working detachment of prisoners living outside a concentration camp

Ausser Dienst
Retired

Bahnschutzpolizei
Railway protection police with auxiliary status. Became part of the SS in 1942

Barbarossa
Code name for the German attack on Russia on the 22nd June 1941

Bauwesen
Branch of the WVHA which controlled forced labour by concentration camp prisoners on works and buildings

Beamter
Functionary

Befehl
Command or order

Befehlshaber der Sicherheitspolizei und des Sicherheitsdienstes
Commander of the Security Police and Security Service in occupied territories

Bekanntmachung
A proclamation

Bewachungsmannschaft
An SS guard detachment in a concentration camp

Berlin Polizei Bureau 1A
Forerunner of the Gestapo

Blockführer
(a) Lowest NSDAP official responsible for the political supervision of 50 households
(b) An SS NCO in charge of a block of concentration camp prisoners

Capo or Kapo
A works foreman of a concentration camp labour force usually a common as opposed to a political criminal

Chef der Sicherheitspolizei und des SD
Chief of the Security Police and Security Service. Heydrich to 1942 then Kaltenbrunner

Chefsache
Top Secret document

Deutsche Ausrüstungswerke
Equipment factory established by the SS in 1939

Deutsche Sportabzeichen
Nazi sports certificate

Deutsche Erd und Steinwerke GmbH
Brickworks company set up by the SS in 1938 using forced labour

Deutsche Rotes Kreuz
German Red Cross controlled indirectly by the SS

Dienstvorschrift
Regulation or a service manual

Durchgangslager
Transit camp

Ehrenführer
Honorary SS general

Einheit
A unit

Einsatzgruppe
An operational task force of the SD and Sipo for special missions into occupied territory

Endlösung, die
The Final Solution. The name used for the mass killing of the Jews

Ersatzheer
The replacement army

Feldlagerkorps
Shock group of the SA disbanded in 1935 and incorporated into the police

Flüchtlingslager
Refugee camp

Fordernde Mitglieder der SS
Patron member of the SS paying regular contributions to SS funds

Freiwilliger
A volunteer

Führer
A leader

Führerhauptquartier
Hitler's field HQ

Führungshauptamt
The operations department of the SS in charge of the organisation and employment of its formations

Gaue
The main territorial unit of the NSDAP Germany was divided into 42 Gaue. The Auslands-Organisation was the 43rd

Gauleiter
NSDAP official in charge of a Gaue Responsible for civil all economic and political affairs, civil defence and the organisation of labour

Geheime Staatspolizei
See Gestapo

Geheimes Staatspolizeiamt
See Gestapa

Gendarmerie
Rural Police, including motorised unit for traffic control

Germanische SS
The Germanic formations of the Waffen SS

Gestapo
The Secret State Police of the RSHA

Gestapa
The National HQ of the Gestapo became part of RSHA in 1939

Gewerbepolizei
Control of trade establishments and the application of price controls

Grenzpolizei or Grepo
Frontier control police, controlled by the SD, they wore SS uniform

Grenzüberwachung
SSG units which reinforced the Grenzpolizei, disbanded in 1937 and absorbed into the Grepo

Häftling
A prisoner

Hakenkreuz
The swastika, emblem of the Nazi party. From 1935 the emblem of the Third Reich

Hauptamt SS
Central office of the SS responsible for welfare, education, recruitment and training of the SS

Hauptamt SS Gericht
Legal department responsible for SS law and discipline within the SS

Haupttreuhandstelle Ost
A public corporation which organised the seizure of Jewish and Polish property, created by Göring

Heer
Army

Hilfsgrenzangestellte
Pre 1939 auxiliary frontier personnel used to reinforce the customs service

Hilfspolizei or Hipo
SS and SA men deputized into the regular police force

Hitler Jugend or HJ
The Hitler Youth formed in 1935 from the junior branch of the SA

Höherer SS und Polizeiführer
Senior SS and Police commander of a Werhkreis

Hoheitsabzeichen
National Badge, the Nazi eagle worn on the left arm of the police and the SS, and on the right breast of the Wehrmacht

Hoheitsträger
A Nazi party official

Iz-Dienst
Intelligence Service of the SS, started by Heydrich, the forerunner of the SD

Jagdverbände
SS sabotage units employed in occupied territories. Its chief was Otto Skorenzy

Junkerschule
An officer cadet training school for the SS

Kasernierte Polizei
Militarised barrack police

Kommandoführer
NCO in charge of a party of prisoners working outside a concentration camp

Konzentrationslager
Concentration camp

Kreis
Administrative district within a Gaue

Kriesleiter
The lowest paid official of the Nazi party. Responsible for a Kries

Kriegsgefangener
A prisoner of war

Kriminalpolizei or Kripo
The criminal police, which with the Gestapo, formed the Security Police (Sipo). Became the Amt V of the RSHA in 1939

Lager
A camp

Lagerkommandant
The chief officer of a concentration camp

Landwacht
Auxiliary rural police established in 1942 to help the regular police. Mostly ex servicemen from the Great War

Lebensborn
Fount of Life maternity homes for both married and unmarried mothers of SS fathered children. Promoted Nazi racial ideas. Paid for by deductions from SS men's pay, single men paying most

Leibstandarte SS Adolf Hitler
Hitler's bodyguard regiment, it was the first militarized SS formation. Formed in 1933 from the Stabswache Berlin, it reached divisional strength in 1941. Fought on the Western and Russian fronts

Leibwache
Bodyguard

Leiter
The leader or chief of an office or authority

Machtergreifung, die
Nazi word for the 'seizure of power' on the 30th January 1933

Max Heiliger
Name of an account in the Reichbank for money made from confiscated valuables and gold teeth of concentration camp inmates

Mitglied
Member

Night and Fog
The title of the order given by the OKW in December 1941. Persons in occupied countries found guilty of any activity against the Third Reich or its representatives, would be deported to Germany. They would be tried by special courts and kept in concentration camps.

Nationalsozialistische Deutsche Arbeiter Partei or NSDAP
The Nazi Party's full title. The National Socialist German Worker's Party

Nationalpolitische Erziehungsanstalten or Napola
National Political Educational Institutes, controlled by the SS and run on Hitler Youth lines. Secondary school level

Nationalsozialistische Kraftfahr-Korps or NSKK
The National Motor Corps, a para-military formation of the Nazi Party

Nationalsozialistische Volkswohlfahrt or NSV
The National Socialist Peoples Welfare Organization

Oberste SA Führer
The supreme commander of the SA. Hitler from 1930, Pfeffer Von Salomon before that

Oberste SA Führung
The High Command of the SA

Persönlicher Stab RfSS
Himmler's Personal Staff, ranking as a Hauptamt of the SS

Politische Leiter
Political leader. A senior official of the Nazi Party

Polizeidivision
A fully militarised formation of the Waffen-SS, established in 1939 from the regular police

Rapportführer
An NCO in the SS responsible for taking roll-calls in a concentration camp

Rasse-und Siedlungshauptamt
The Central Office for Race and Settlement, run by the SS. It was supposed to control the racial purity of the SS and organise the settlement of SS colonists in the conquered eastern territories

Reichführer-SS and Chef der Deutschen Polizei
Reich Chief of the SS and Head of the German Police. A title created for Himmler in 1936

Reichsführung-SS
The Supreme Command of the SS

Reichssicherheitsdienst
A special Security Service for guarding Hitler and the leading members of the Nazi Party. Recruited from the criminal police

Reichssicherheitshauptamt or RSHA
The Central Security Department of the Reich, consisting of the Gestapo, Kripo, and the SD. Established in 1939

Reichskriegsflagge
A voluntary para-military organisation led by Roehm, which joined forces with Hitler during the Munich Putch. It formed the nucleus of the SA or Brownshirts

Sanitätsdienst
Medical Service

Salon Kitty
High class brothel established by Heydrich in Berlin for foreign diplomats and senior Nazi Partymembers. It had nine bedrooms with hidden microphones which were used for gathering incriminating or embarrassing evidence for blackmail or other purposes by Heydrich

Schutzhaft
Protective custody

Schutzhaftlager
Concentration camp

SS Fliegersturm
Formed in Munich in 1931, absorbed into the Deutsche Luftsfort Verbund in
1933

Schutzstaffel
The SS. Literally Protection Detachment, formed in 1925 from the Stosstrupp
Hitler

Selbstschutz
(a) A self help militia recruited by the SS from the Volksdeutsche in Poland
(b) A German nationalist self protection organization. Pre 1925
(c) The self protection service, part of the Luftschutzdienst made up of air
     raid wardens

Sicherheitsdienst des RfSS or SD
The Security Branch of the SS formed in 1932 under Heydrich. The Intelligence Organization of the NSDAP

Sicherheitshauptamt or SD Hauptamt
The SS Central Security Department

Sicherheitspolizei
Security Police. Made up of the Gestapo and the Kripo under Heydrich

Sigrunen
The runic double S insignia of the SS

Sonderkommando
Special detachment of the SS for police and political tasks

Staatsschutzkorps
A semi-official term for the combined functions of the Gestapo, Kripo and
SD for the protection of the state

Stab
A staff

Stabswache
The original Party HQ guard, formed from the SA in 1923 and later merged
into the Stosstrupp Adolf Hitler

Stammlager or Stalag
A permanent prisoner of war camp

Standarte
An SS or SA formation roughly the size of a regiment

Standrecht
Martial law

Stosstrupp
Shock troop

Streifendienst
The Hitler Youth Patrol Service officered by the SS

Sturm
An SS or SA formation roughly the size of a company

Sturmabteilungen
The SA or Brownshirts or Stormtroopers. The original Shocktroops of the NSDAP founded in 1921. It lost its political power to the SS after the 1934 purge. It became responsible for the pre-military training of all able-bodied males in 1939

Sturmbann
An SS or SA formation roughly the size of a battalion

Totenkopfverbände or TV
Death's Heads units. Originally made up of volunteers from the Allgemeine SS. Employed as concentration guards. Formed the nucleus of the first field formations of the Waffen-SS

Verfügungstruppe
The original militarised formations of the SS renamed Waffen SS in 1939

Vernichtungslager
An extermination camp

Vertrauensmann
An intelligence agent or informer

Volksbund für das Deutschtum im Ausland
The league for Germans abroad. A pre Nazi organization taken over by the Party in 1930

Volkskartei
The national register kept by the administrative police

Wachverbände
Original SS concentration camp guards, later became the SS Totenkopfverbände

Waffen SS
The militarized formations of the SS. Originally composed of the Verfügungstruppe and the Totenkopfverbände. Combined non German SS units after 1940

Wirtschafts-und Verwaltungshauptamt
The SS economic and administrative office which controlled the economic enterprise of the SS and administered the concentration camps. It was run by Oswald Pohl

Index

Sources of material

L Milner collection: 18-26, 29, 30, 32, 37, 40, 41, 42, 43, 44, 45, 73, 74, 79, 85, 84, 98, 99, 122

R Smith collection: 27, 28, 33, 35, 36, 38, 52, 53, 60, 61, 71, 73, 75, 77, 80, 81, 87, 127, 128, 130, 131

Imperial War Museum: 31, 37, 39, 42, 54, 55, 66, 67, 70, 72, 76, 82, 83, 86, 100-121, 132, 133, 134, 135

M Lukich collection: 33, 56, 57, 58, 59, 62, 63, 64, 65, 126

Musée de Trois Guerres,Châteaudun,France: 46, 47, 92, 93

Musée de l'Armée,Brussels,Belgium: 68, 69, 78

C Farlowe: 34

Acknowledgements

I would like to thank Laurie Milner, the uniform curator of the Imperial War Museum London, for his help in the preparation of this book: also for the help and advice given by the Musée de la Guerre, Paris; The Bundersarchiv, Koblenz; The Musée de l'Armée, Brussels; The Musée de Trois Guerres, Châteaudun; Major F Wicksworth; and J R Daniels

Editor-in-Chief: Barrie Pitt
Art Director: Sarah Kingham
Editor: David Mason
Cover/Design: Dave Allen
Illustrations: Graham Bingham